More Than BIRDING

Observations from Antarctica, Madagascar and Bhutan

Harriet Denison

Peace Corps Writers
Oakland, California

More Than Birding

Subtitle of book: Observations from Antarctica,
Madagascar and Bhutan

ISBN 9781935925972

An Imprint of Peace Corps Worldwide

Book Designer: Sherry Wachter
Website: www.travelswithharriet.org

For more information, contact peacecorpsworld-
wide@gmail.com. Peace Corps Writers and the
Peace Corps Writers colophon are trademarks of
PeaceCorpsWorldwide.org.

Library of Congress Control Number: (To Come)

First Peace Corps Writers Edition, (Info to come)

Why I Travel

We travel, initially, to lose ourselves; and we travel, next, to find ourselves. We travel to open our hearts and eyes and learn more about the world than our newspapers will accommodate. We travel to bring what little we can, in our ignorance and knowledge, to those parts of the globe whose riches are differently dispersed. And we travel, in essence, to become young fools again — to slow time down and get taken in, and fall in love once more. The beauty of this whole process was best described, perhaps, before people even took to frequent flying, by George Santayana in his lapidary essay, "The Philosophy of Travel." We "need sometimes," the Harvard philosopher wrote, "to escape into open solitudes, into aimlessness, into the moral holiday of running some pure hazard, in order to sharpen the edge of life, to taste hardship, and to be compelled to work desperately for a moment at no matter what."

Pico Iyer
Salon Travel *Contributing Editor*
EXCERPTED FROM HIS ARTICLE
"WHY WE TRAVEL"

Contents

Evolution of a Birder

Birding offers more than just seeing a new species of bird to add to a list. In fact, most people who have observed a few birds soon discover that they are not just "watching" birds at all. They are listening for songs, looking for field marks, and noting behaviors like flight patterns or how the bird sits on a branch or dives into the water.

Nearly twenty years ago, I began birding and enjoyed finding and naming the local birds, but I knew there were more possibilities. After my first birding tour outside the United States, I realized birding tours were a great way to continue my frequent travels but with a focus that took me off the usual tourist routes. Birding is a low impact way to enjoy natural environments while supporting local conservation efforts. More importantly, birding fills my need for an intense experience with the natural world—and international birding trips deliver in spades.

When the avian activity slows down on a trip, I find myself as interested in what is around me as I am in the birds; the landscape, its plants and animals—even the local fungi. I never tire of the fascinating complexity of the natural world and its inhabitants in all forms. My brief encounters with the local people, their culture, politics, and history often lead me to diverse queries during and after my trips.

A terrific biology teacher in high school, Calvin Foulk, piqued my interest in all living things and helped me begin to organize my thoughts about the natural world. In college, I envied the humanities students who could take a semester abroad. Chemistry majors like me did not have that opportunity. However, a summer work project in Malawi in central Africa with other college students screamed my name and I signed up. That formative summer led to my Peace Corps experience teaching biology in Tanzania, drawing on what I learned in my high school class. During my time in Tanzania, I was always alert for new living creatures to study, so much so that one morning some of my Tanzanian students ran breathlessly to tell me they had found a snake in Mrs. Berry's garden on Lake Victoria. Having dealt with rattlesnakes native to my home state of Oregon, I killed the snake and preserved the skin for the biology lab collection. Later, I identified it as one of the poisonous snakes, a Black Mamba as I recall, common but not often seen. (My Peace Corps work lead to the writing of my second book, *Leopards at My Door: Peace Corps, Tanzania, 1966—1967*, published by Peace Corps Writers 2014).

Previous to my interest in birding, my passion had been scuba diving, exploring ocean rocks and reefs. On my last scuba diving trip to the Solomon Islands in 1998, I lurked, weightless, above the reef and watched the colorful fish carry on with their lives. Between my gurgled exhalations, I enjoyed the clicks, grunts, and groans from various fish and even heard some whale songs. The names of the sea creatures were secondary although I did try to identify the few I could remember after I climbed back onto the dive boat. Usually any details I had garnered while scuba diving were soon forgotten once I was on the boat, which I found frustrating given my inquisitive nature. By this time, I was in my mid-50s and becoming acutely aware of the amount of heavy scuba diving equipment I had to haul around with me as a diver.

Over time, my personal library of reference books for fish, birds, wildflowers, butterflies, and so many other topics grew to support my interest in all living things, but still, I lacked a systematic approach to identification. For example, if I saw an interesting bird, I'd thumb through my bird guide looking for what had just flown away. It was frustrating but occasionally fruitful. After a five-day birding tour with the Portland Audubon Society in the Malheur region of southeastern Oregon in 2000, I finally felt comfortable using a field guide to identify a bird. During that tour, I learned the similarities of birds in various families and thus, where to begin looking in my field guide for more information about the bird. The natural world began to make orderly sense.

After that week with the skilled Audubon staff, I thought, *At least I know something about bird families and field marks.* Then I got excited with the possibilities.

There was so much to learn! I was far from feeling competent when I began birding in serious, but I understood that there was a method to identification. Watching birds delighted me to no end, whether they were flying, hammering on a tree trunk, eating a tasty seed or worm, or singing with abandon. *Yes, birds are in a world worth investigating.*

During that first intense birding trip in Oregon, I realized that birding filled that nature niche and happily, the equipment I needed was minimal: ears to listen for the birdsongs, eyes to catch their movements, and binoculars for closer observations of bird life. After that first birding tour in May 2000, I hung up my wetsuit and focused on birding for my natural high.

As a newbie birder, my first goal was to learn the birds of my own region, anticipating travel far afield later. I thought it would be too embarrassing to be with knowledgeable birders far from home and ask the name of some bird common in Oregon. For almost two years, I went out with Audubon groups in every season, learning my local birds. As I gained confidence to go out alone, I discovered how practical my small sixteen-foot RV was for birding. It had all I needed to travel around Oregon and find birds not common in Portland. My RV also served as a very good blind to observe birds without being seen. Birds did not see my van as a threat, so I could get quite close. *How exciting!* I thought, *I can sit in the front seat with a cup of coffee and watch the birds going about their business unaware I was observing them. Nothing better.*

That fall after the Audubon workshop, I loaded my binoculars and telescope into my van that I had named

Turtle. Travelling by myself, I meandered for two months across the United States and on to Nova Scotia, Canada and then back to Oregon. It was thrilling to see birds that rarely visited my home state, but were common and easily seen in other places. I concluded that going where they were in abundance was the easiest way to find birds, which vaulted me into several years of international birding trips.

Antarctica had been on my bucket list long before there was such a concept as a "bucket list." Years earlier I had read that the residents at the remote Argentinian station in Antarctica threw their garbage on a penguin colony, and that cruise ships dumped their sewage into the water. This really bothered me and I was hesitant to join a tour that might further trash Antarctica—but I reconsidered in the spring of 2001 when Portland Audubon advertised a November trip to Antarctica. I signed up right away. I knew that if the Audubon staff made the arrangements, things must have changed regarding the protection of the birds. The combination of birding while knowing the environment was protected was irresistible. While waiting for that first international trip, I stretched my birding experiences with a tour to Southeastern Arizona with Portland Audubon and a tour to South Texas with Mark Smith Nature Tours.

Following my spectacular trip to Antarctica, I kept up my local birding along with a few other trips in the United States, including a birding trip to Florida with a friend. The Florida trip was fun but we were both new to birding and it was frustrating. I decided organized trips like the Antarctica guided tour worked better for me. Birding friends recommended Field Guides, a well-respected birding tour company, as a possibility for future trips. My tour to Cape May, New Jersey with Field Guides' Megan Crewe convinced me that this was a company worth using for future trips. Since then, I have done most of my birding trips with them.

Over the next twelve years I did fourteen international birding trips to far away places in addition to other non-birding trips. Three of those extraordinary journeys are found in the pages of this book. Antarctica was a good start into my foray of international birding, followed by quite a number of remote places that called to me: Madagascar, Bhutan, Papua New Guinea, Borneo, and the Amazon Basin, among others. The long plane trips to reach these destinations half way around the world were tiring, so I resolved to see as many of the far, far away places while I still had the energy. My plan was to do the closer and less rugged destinations later. Thus, my earlier decision to begin with a trip to Antarctica fit in nicely!

On my return home from some birding trips, I wrote about things that caught my attention, whether it was a single incident or a recurring theme that I noted during the trip. On every trip there were birds with their peculiarities and exquisite uniqueness, along with unrelated surprises in addition to birding. Realizing how fortunate I was to see these places firsthand, I made a point to write about the most unusual destinations and events to share with others.

I loved writing about my experiences, reliving the details, straining for just the right way to express what

I saw, felt, heard, experienced. And I have continued to love the writing as I read and research related topics once I was home, expanding and enriching my own understanding of the places I've been.

More Than Birding is partly about the birds and the hunt for them and a lot about other things. Readers will learn about Antarctica, Madagascar, and Bhutan, along with odd tangential ideas not considered by the hardcore birder who only wants to snag another bird for their life list.

At first, I envisioned narratives from eight countries in a book, but after reveling in the writing of these three, a single book emerged. Other stories will follow.

—*Harriet Denison*
JULY 20 18

Antarctica

2001

Routes crossing Drake Passage

TIERRA DEL FUEGO and the
ANTARCTIC PENINSULA

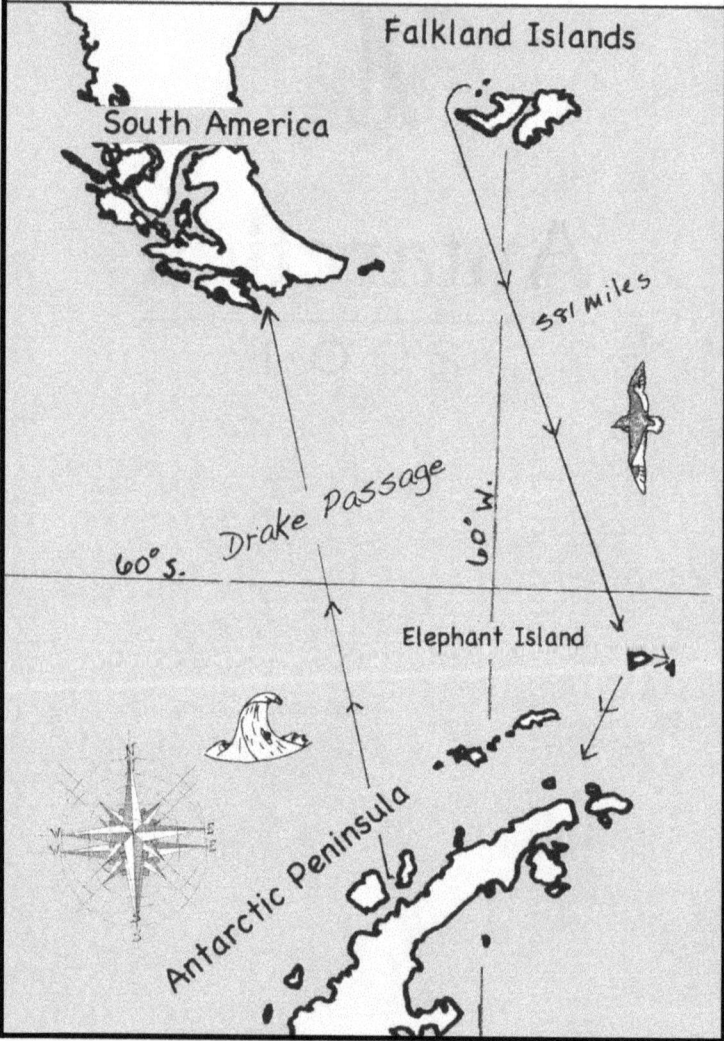

Falkland Islands

South America

581 miles

Drake Passage

60°S.

60°W.

Elephant Island

Antarctic Peninsula

Map by Harriet Denison

Introduction

In high school, I had read *Endurance:Shackleton's Incredible Voyage* by Alfred Lansing, first published in 1959. When I learned about this dramatic exploration, my imagination went wild. I have always loved true adventure stories and this account of Sir Ernest Shackleton's expedition was riveting. The descriptions of Antarctica and its severe polar conditions fired up my curiosity about such an exotic place.

In Shackelton's day, all of the "firsts" of exploration in Antarctica had been claimed except for one: crossing the entire continent. Shackleton resolved to do just that—to cross the continent from the Weddell Sea to the South Pole and on to the Ross Sea. However, in 1914 Shackleton and his 27 crew members soon faced daunting challenges that brought them to the brink of death, yet they all survived after almost 17 months in Antarctica's frozen landscape. The following description from the Shackleton Exhibit at the American Museum of Natural History sums up the expedition:

Sir Ernest Shackleton's 1914 Voyage to the Antarctic

Just one day's sail from the continent [of Antarctica], the ship Endurance became trapped in sea ice. Frozen fast for ten months, the ship was crushed and destroyed by ice pressure, and the crew was forced to abandon ship. After camping on the ice for five months, Shackleton made two open boat journeys, one of which—a treacherous 800-mile ocean crossing to South Georgia Island—is now considered one of the greatest boat journeys in history. Trekking across the mountains of South Georgia, Shackleton reached the island's remote whaling station, organized a rescue team, and saved all of the men he had left behind.

Ever since reading that book I have thought, *What an amazing journey.* Not a single man died on the expedition during the many months of freezing weather, starvation, and isolation in Antarctica. In my own life during difficult times, I would recall Shackleton's story and this gave me courage to push myself and prevail.

Prior to Shackleton's expedition, only whalers and a few explorers had touched the shores of this frozen continent. Some died there, but most sailed for home after only a brief stay of weeks or months. For years after Shackleton's Antarctica expedition, only a handful of researchers and the last of the old-time whalers ventured to the area. However, in the mid-20th century, travel to Antarctica increased and human impact on the once isolated landscape became a problem. I had read that some of the research stations dumped their refuse on penguin colonies, which I found distressing. When the first sizable tourist cruises ventured to Antarctica in the 1960s, they threw their trash off the ships. Both discoveries shocked me deeply and I vowed to not contribute to its degradation. Although I had wanted to see this continent for most of my life and get a firsthand sense of this strange land, I lost hope that I could ever visit Antarctica.

All of that changed when my local Audubon Society in Portland, Oregon scheduled a trip to Antarctica for November 2001. For me, the timing for this trip was excellent. Birding had recently captivated me and I knew the Audubon Society had the integrity to schedule a trip with a touring company that respected the wildlife there.

Falkland Islands

On November 19, 2001, I flew with 22 fellow birders from Portland to the Falkland Islands where the polar expedition vessel, The Clipper Adventurer (now named The Sea Adventurer) waited to take some 75 passengers to Antarctica. My fellow birders and I were still reeling from the devastating 9/11 terrorist attacks on the United States, which influenced many tourists to cancel their Antarctic trip. However, those of us who decided to still go looked forward to a respite from the unending news of this tragedy. We hoped we could find peace and beauty on this remote continent far from civilization and its madness.

The Falkland Islands is known as the gateway to Antarctica since so many ships bound for the frozen continent stop here first. The impending visit piqued my curiosity to learn more about this archipelago made up of more than 700 small islands and two main islands. Before my trip, I had only known the Falklands as some islands in the ocean east of South America where Great Britain and Argentina fought the Falklands War in 1982. I was excited to visit the Falklands since few people make it to this little known archipelago. I have always liked exploring remote and exotic places because I like surprises—not the "Surprise! Happy Birthday" kind, but surprises that are strange and unfamiliar, and shake up my knowledge of the world and what I know.

Argentina calls the islands *Las Islas Malvinas* and still disputes the outcome of the war in 1982. Because of that ongoing dispute, our once-a-week flight in 2001 to the Falklands originated in Santiago, Chile, instead of Buenos Aires, Argentina, even though Buenos Aires was much closer to our destination. As of 2015, tourists still must fly from Santiago through Punta Arenas to reach Mt. Pleasant International Airport in the Falklands.

Getting to Antarctica

Wealthy tourists can fly to Antarctica, but most visitors go by ship, leaving either from the Falkland Islands, or from Ushuaia, Tierra del Fuego in Argentina. All ships have to cross Drake Passage, a body of water with a mean reputation. That sounded like my kind of adventure!

Antarctica is the southernmost continent on Earth with the South Pole at the center—the point from which everywhere else is north. British explorer Roald

Amundson was the first to reach the South Pole in 1911. Surrounded by the Southern Ocean, Antarctica is twice the size of Australia and is the only continent to double its size in the winter when ice forms on the bays and harbors. Most of the rocky continent is covered with ice over one mile thick. Only about two inches of snow fall annually on the interior of Antarctica, but it never melts due to the never ending cold. Even though 98% of Antarctica is covered by ice, it is considered a desert because so little rain or snow falls. Most of the moisture accumulates on the edges, near the open water. The wildlife that thrives in Antarctica includes several species of sea birds, penguins, seals, whales, and krill, the tiny shrimp that feeds them all.

All maps of Earth are oriented with north at the top. Since everywhere from the South Pole is north, a topographical convention has emerged that places the Antarctic Peninsula on the left side of the Antarctica map. This peninsula is a long narrow triangle of land reaching northward about 800 miles from the west side of the continent. The Antarctic Peninsula forms the western edge of the Weddell Sea where Ernest Shackleton struggled to save the lives of his crew.

The Antarctic Peninsula is the most popular destination for ships, carrying up to 200 passengers at a time, curious to see this remote land. Only a small number of visitors actually set foot on the continent itself, so I looked forward to being one of them. Many penguins breed on this peninsula and the islands offshore because it is the northern most part of Antarctica where the ice melts earliest in the year. Birds are plentiful at the edges Antarctica, but there are relatively few species represented. Personally, I didn't care—I just wanted to see Antarctica and of course, the penguins.

Unlike the early explorers, many of whom died or spent months living in miserable rock huts awaiting rescue, I admit I like a little comfort on my adventures. Good food, a warm bed, and hot water are more my style, but nothing extravagant. This Audubon trip sounded perfect for me.

After reading *Endurance,* I only imagined that one day I might actually set eyes on Antarctica's white and icy splendor, and witness its desolation; to breathe the same air as Shackleton's crew and to gaze at the wide sky they had so much time to ponder as they waited for rescue. Never would I have thought I might watch breeding activities of penguins who are descendants of the colonies that Shackleton's men once hunted during the many months they survived on penguins for sustenance and fuel.

At last, I would get to experience this remote continent at the bottom of the earth.

Harriet in downtown Stanley, capital of the Falkland Islands

First Stop, Falkland Islands

The bleak landscape of East Falkland Island came into clear view as I pressed my cheek against the plane's cold window, surveying this remote island. Scrubby bushes peppered rugged hillsides and one paved road dribbled off over a rise. Next to a few lonely airport buildings at Mount Pleasant Military Complex, a British flag flapped straight out, caught in a stiff wind. I had waited a long time to realize this dream trip and at last, it had begun.

Yay! I'm so close to one of the most remote places on earth. Next stop, Antarctica!

When our plane touched down, my spirits rose. No more plane rides. It had been a long haul to reach this remote place. When we stepped onto the tarmac, the British term for asphalt, a balmy summer wind whipped our clothes and hair. Since the seasons are reversed in the southern hemisphere, it was a nice change from the chilly November weather back home in Portland, Oregon. The British Royal Air Force had built this small international airport after the Falklands War in 1982. The friction with Argentina over the possession of these islands remained after the brief war, so to protect the Falklanders who are mostly British, they made the airport part of a military complex located 37 miles from the capital, Stanley.

My first impressions of the Falklands were fuzzy after our two-and-a-half-day trip from Oregon. My only break occurred with a brief layover in Santiago, Chile where I saw my first Andean Condor sailing high above a ski resort at the end of a steep mountain road. It was a most impressive sight.

After landing, we rode on a small bus for half an hour toward Stanley, home to most of the Falkland inhabitants. The landscape looked barren, but our chatty bus driver pointed out the short shrub heath and the tall tussock grass, a coarse white grass with broad leaves that thrashes in strong breezes. The bus driver told us her family heats their house with peat, the partially decomposed tussock grass that forms in acidic swamps, abundant in the Falkland Islands. The acidic swamps are also the reason why there are no native trees. The few farms we passed sat near well-grazed pastures, and depended on prickly gorse planted around the houses and barns to break the near constant wind.

Occasionally, formations called stone runs or stone rivers, broke the monotony of the landscape. They are a curiosity found throughout the Falklands and scientists have studied them for years. When granite froze and thawed repeatedly during the last Ice Age, this geological activity created the stone runs by breaking apart the rock and rounding the edges into smaller chunks. The runs have the appearance of water seeping down the gullies, only instead of water there are heaps of rounded stones that form a flowing pattern.

Our First Falkland Birds

The polar expedition ship, Clipper Adventurer, waited in the next bay east of Stanley. The crew prepared for our arrival while all the passengers stopped for lunch in Stanley. This left us plenty of time to see the quaint and very British capital that was only a block long.

For a birder, the best thing about travel is that you can easily see birds that are locally abundant in a new environment, but often scarce or nonexistent elsewhere in the world. This was true in the Falklands, which is home to 59 bird species that habitually breed on the islands. Most of them are water birds.

Directly across the street from the Upland Goose Hotel, our lunch stop, a finger of the sea stretched toward the town, creating an ideal spot for water birds to congregate along the shoreline. Several unfamiliar birds immediately drew the attention of my Portland Audubon group.

This was my first international birding trip and I knew I had a lot to learn, so I shuffled up close to the three birders who seemed to know the names of the birds on the water. A birder named Bill pointed to quite a large gull that fluttered a foot above the shallow water. After the third shallow dive, the bird came up with a small snail and flew off. Bill noted, "Kelp Gull. Found only in the southern hemisphere. We'll see that further south."

"Oh, look," another birder exclaimed, jutting his chin toward a small grey goose with a brownish head walking along the shore. "That's a Ruddy-headed Goose. Threatened and most of them live here in the Falklands."

"A steamer-duck," another birder quietly chimed in, loud enough for us to pass on to the others in a very soft voice so as not to spook the bird.

"Boy, it sure is, but which one?" John agreed. "Both the Falklands Steamer-duck and the Flying Steamer-duck live here."

A pair of dark grey ducks floating on the water became the subject of the birders' discussion about field marks and behaviors. Their observations boiled down to, "If only that duck would fly, we would know if it's the flying steamer-duck and not the Falkland steamer duck, but even they don't like to fly in spite of their name."

Maybe annoyed by the discussion, the two birds suddenly jumped up and churned their way ten feet out into the water as if trying to fly, but not quite taking off. The splashy and frantic movements reminded me of a paddle steamer.

"Well, that's what steamer-ducks do, but it didn't help with the I.D.," Bill sighed.

The experts got out their books and I listened while they tried to determine which duck we were observing.

Steamer-ducks have shorter than usual wings and are quite heavy, easily up to ten pounds. Scientists are still debating whether their weight evolved before or after the evolutionary change in their shortened wing-span, which rendered all but one species flightless.

My brain soon filled with birding minutiae and refused to take in any more. So, I pulled away from the discussion to watch those rare and peculiar ducks paddling around in their home territory. I felt jittery with glee; the breeze on my face, the sun on my back, and standing in a remote place far from the crowds. Perfect.

My stomach grumbled. As I passed the experts on my way to the hotel, I overheard one of them say that he knew a researcher who studied steamer-ducks. While out in the field one day, the researcher stepped too close to a pair of the ducks and got a good crack on his shin. These flightless ducks defend themselves by using two keratinized knobs that grow on the middle joint of their wings, great for whacking a potential threat. That researcher got a firsthand experience with those wings. I studied the ducks for a moment longer looking at their wings, but their red knobs were tucked under their feathers.

The Upland Goose Hotel put on a luncheon spread for all 75 of the eager Antarctic passengers who arrived in waves, our Audubon group among them. The buffet overflowed with creative dishes. The scent of baked bread and sweets fresh out of the oven wafted through the dining area with a yeasty fragrance. We feasted on several kinds of quiche, baked fish covered with cucumber slices, potato salads, and green salads trimmed with sliced hard-boiled eggs. We may have been on a remote island far from urban comforts, but this buffet was as plentiful and savory as any culinary spread in a good restaurant back home. The hotel employee keeping the platters replenished explained that some local farmers built green houses on the island that defy the winds and cool weather in order to provide an ample bounty during the tourist season, their summer months from October to April.

War & Land Mines

After lunch, I decided to visit the Land Mine Museum situated near the Upland Goose Hotel. The Falklanders had built this museum after their war with Argentina and I wanted to learn more about this little understood conflict.

Walking along the picturesque waterfront felt divine, a great way to stretch my legs. Caught up in the moment, I almost passed the obscure small museum. Once inside the dark lobby, I studied the displays that explained the history of the 72-day war. Great Britain first claimed the Falkland Islands in 1690 and then lost control to Spain. Britain reclaimed the archipelago in 1833 and installed a governor, which initiated the first permanent settlement. Argentina is physically the closest country and the logical claimant, and has disputed for years Great Britain's sovereignty. Some say that internal unrest in Argentina spurred the invasion of the Falklands on April 2, 1982 after claiming the islands as theirs, again.

During the war, troops from both Britain and Argentina planted almost twenty thousand land mines throughout the islands, including thousands along the coastline near Stanley, thus the reason for this little museum. Great Britain prevailed and after the short war, the few attempts to disarm the landmines resulted in too many injuries. The British military fenced off the 117 minefields and set up the Land Mine Museum to educate the townspeople on how to recognize and deal with mines they might find in the ground. At the museum, a dim display of about a dozen types of landmines included labels with each mine's name and its potential dangers. The heavy mines, often buried in the soft peat, could still be dangerous years later to anyone digging in the peat.

Restricting access to the minefields had been a boon for the shrinking penguin population. During the whaling years, workers used penguin bodies as fuel to render whale blubber, diminishing the penguin population. In more recent years, overfishing in the area depleted the penguins' food supply, further devastating their numbers. But penguins are not heavy enough to set off the land mines, so they have survived in areas where people, cows, and sheep have been prohibited for their own safety. I love that this unintended outcome of the war benefitted the penguins nicely.

Economic Survival

Archeologists have not identified any artifacts indicating that indigenous people lived on this land. The only signs of human existence in the Falklands are from people who came to the islands in more recent centuries. Since the 1700s, ships stopped at the Falklands for supplies and repairs. Whalers on their way to Antarctica stopped, as did trade vessels preparing to round the tip of South America.

From the beginning, Falklanders have led a hard and lonely existence. The current inhabitants are all transplants, mostly rugged British settlers. The first permanent settlers arrived after Great Britain installed a governor in 1833. Britain established a land-based whaling station there in 1909 to process whale blubber for oil, but the small number of whales in the area did not support the whaling station. The hunters added elephant seals and penguins to the rendering vats, but the numbers still proved inadequate. Britain opened another processing plant on the South Georgia Islands and closed the one in the Falklands in 1915, leaving the workers to find other ways to survive.

Many islanders consider the 1982 war as the event that defined the beginning of the Falklands' modern history. At the time of the war, fewer than 2,000 people lived in the Falklands permanently, mostly on East Falkland Island in and around Stanley. When we visited in 2001, the population was 3,053, which did not include contractors and military people living on the island temporarily.

Products from sheep continue to be important to the economy of the Falklands, and income from fishing and tourism is increasing. After the war, the burgeoning interest in Antarctica prompted the arrival of huge ocean liners full of tourists that stopped in Stanley on the way south. In the year I visited, more than 22,000 tourists passed through. Some tourists came to see the remnants of the Falklands War; while others were on their way to Antarctica.

East Falkland Island

After everyone finished a hearty lunch, our group enjoyed a quick tour around East Falkland Island to see more of the surrounding environs and learn more about the residents. Our local guide told us she fell in love with the Falklands when she arrived on a cruise ship in 1980, and decided to move to the island. During our visit, her family was one of the few still heating their home with peat, the only local and plentiful source of fuel. She helped her family cut peat blocks out of the bogs and stack them for drying. Our guide noted that burning peat formed from tussock grass smells like burning hair, which is probably why the rest of the island's inhabitants switched to oil for heating. The imported oil is pricier, but less work to obtain and emits no unpleasant odors.

On our tour, we passed small settlements, some consisting of one farmer's house and outbuildings, protected from the wind by head-high, prickly gorse. Beyond the wind barrier grew additional thick clumps of tussock grass we had seen all day on the barren, windswept expanses. Fitzroy is one of the settlements, and is located on the ring of roads that touch the battlefield sites throughout East Falkland Island. During the war, Fitzroy had been the site of Britain's greatest blunder. During an air fight that left their base unprotected, 51 soldiers died and nearly 100 were injured. That story reminded me of our Civil War stories where elderly ladies watched the battles from their farmhouse windows. I wondered, *Did those remote Falklanders stay for the battle, or did they wisely seek the safety of Stanley?* Our guide had so much to tell us that I didn't get a chance to ask her about that.

As I often do, I tried to imagine myself living there. With such a small population, everybody would know everyone's business—something that made me feel uncomfortable. On the other hand, the community would be tight, tolerant, and helpful since they all had to depend on each other. I have enjoyed living in communities like that for short periods of time, which was enough for me.

In a small bay out of sight from the town, we climbed off our small bus where our ship waited at the pier. At last, we were about to embark on our journey to Antarctica!

The Carcass Island homestead, Falkland Islands.

CHAPTER 2

Our First Shore Excursions

Imagine my relief to discover that *Clipper Adventurer*, our home for the next twelve days, was relatively small for a cruise ship. I'd seen photos of her, but I also had stood next to one of the mega-cruise ships docked in Portland on the Willamette River near where I paddle dragon boats. These ocean cruisers often have ten-passenger decks and accommodations for more than 3,000 people, the size of a small city. I could barely breathe thinking of all the people wandering around on that huge ship, worse than a city because they could not leave town for the weekend.

At 133-feet long, *Clipper Adventurer* held only 120 passengers. Not all of them showed up because our tour took place about two months after the attack on the World Trade Center on 9/11. A smaller group of passengers was icing on the cake in my mind. All my residual anxiety faded when I realized I did not have to fight a crowd to eat, or find a seat for lectures, or get a spot on a shore boat. Also, I was reassured knowing *Clipper Adventurer* had been built for travel in Polar

Regions with stabilizers for the rough seas and a reinforced hull, sturdy enough to bump aside small chunks of ice.

Once on board, a crewmember showed me to my cozy room in the bowels of the ship where my red jacket awaited me, placed conspicuously on my bed. The photos I'd seen of tours to Antarctica always showed people in bright red jackets. When I signed up for the tour, I found out I would receive my own red jacket when I boarded the ship. I expected the weather would be so harsh that no jacket I owned would be good enough. Images of the explorers one hundred years earlier with icicles dripping off their beards caused me to put my faith in our ship's provisioner. I trusted he would know best what we needed to survive. My jacket's bright red fabric made of a sturdy material would cut the wind well and I loved the fleece lining since I am so often cold. When I tried it on, I really knew I was on my way to Antarctica.

Our tour guides did not mention that we might not need our red jackets for every outing. When we boarded the ship in the Falkland Islands, we wore light jackets from home against the stiff breeze, but the daytime noon temperature was 66° F, a pleasant summer day for the area. Despite the mild weather I thought, *Here I am in the Antarctic,* (Technically, we weren't quite there yet.) *I'll need this heavier jacket.*

Thinking about it now, I have to laugh about my affinity for my red jacket!

In time, I learned that the red jackets had a dual purpose; in addition to warmth they allowed the crew to keep better track of us on land. From the ship, the duty crewperson could see our little red spots and radio someone on shore if a problem arose. Our bright red showed up quite well against bare rocks or snow, especially when we reached the Antarctic Peninsula. We had heard the story of one tourist who had decided to commit suicide by walking away from the group and staying on shore, but his red jacket gave him away. During our day excursions on land no one wandered far from the group, but there were times when some people found it difficult to obey the rule to stay fifteen feet away from wildlife. When we reached Antarctica, I only heard a naturalist shout out once to a red figure on the next ridge creeping too close to a cluster of penguins, his camera poised for the photo of a lifetime.

While we slept that first night on board *Clipper Adventurer,* the captain navigated the ship about 160 miles north and west around the archipelago from Stanley and anchored off Carcass Island. This seven-square-mile island is located in the northern most collection of tiny islands that are part of the Falklands. At breakfast on the ship we spotted our first penguins, only small dots on the distant shore that wobbled like penguins. What a thrill to see them in their own environment, so different from those confined in a zoo. I couldn't wait to see them up close!

Penguins Up Close

We soon boarded rubber Zodiacs that shuttled us ashore ten at a time to Carcass Island. Cheered by the sun, the howling wind and small white caps did not deter us. Julio Preller, our landing boss, pointed out Magellanic penguins scattered among the shore grasses that looked as if they were greeting our arrival. Many of them stood on humps of tussock grass that hid and protected their burrows dug into the roots of the tough grass. Like all penguins, they had black backs and white fronts, but the extra black stripe across the chest of these Magellenic penguins distinguished them from other penguins. In time, I would be able to easily distinguish between the various species.

Once our boat reached the shore, Julio and his crew held the Zodiac's fat sides steady and helped us out. We waded ashore in the ankle-deep water and once on shore, changed from our waterproof boots into hiking shoes. Julio reminded us when the last boat would return to the ship and then left us on our own to explore.

Nearby, a Magellenic Oystercatcher with a long red bill, a black head and back, and a white belly, foraged for food seemingly undisturbed by our presence. The red jackets ahead of us showed the way. We plunged into the sea of tussock grass, following the trail toward the island's one farmhouse. On either side of the trail nesting Gentoo Penguins watched us, unperturbed. The pairs had constructed nests of sticks, feathers, and grass. At each nest, one penguin stood to the side, often braying to the sky like a hoarse donkey. The other parent lay gently on the chicks to keep them warm. Gentoos are one of the larger penguin species, up to thirty-five inches in height, about waist high if I could have gotten close enough to measure. They have a bright orange bill and a wide white strip across the top of the head.

Several globally endangered but locally plentiful Striated Caracara glided over our heads. This bird of prey feeds on carrion, so they nest near penguin and albatross colonies, ideal spots for finding a meal. Most penguin chicks had already hatched that spring and the caracara watched with hungry eyes for unguarded chicks.

Rob and Lorraine McGill, owners of Carcass Island since 1974, awaited our arrival at their farmhouse. The McGills had teatime for 75 people down to an art. People from the ship arrived in small groups, enjoyed the McGills' hospitality, and then left as the next wave of visitors arrived. The hosts welcomed all of us with smiles, poured tea and warm milk, and refilled plates of cookies until all the stragglers finished their tea.

Our genial host Rob answered our questions about island living. "Well, you have to be self-sufficient and be able to repair most anything. It's difficult to bring heavy bags of feed or fertilizer over from Stanley, so if we need to, we can hire a small boat." Laughing, Rob noted, "Animals are the most difficult, you can imagine they don't like to ride on a wobbly boat."

"What about a medical emergency?" I asked because I have lived on an island and that is one of the disadvantages of the isolation.

"In a real emergency, we can get a military helicopter to come from Stanley, but that's pricey and we aren't rich here. I have a little boat I use for some of the trips. Usually we use my jeep to get to where we keep our boat. It's pretty bouncy and sometimes we get stuck in the soggy peat, but we make do." He added, "If we just need to get around the island to check fences and so forth, we can use horses to travel across the soggy landscape."

I had to chuckle to myself as I listened to Rob describe his love of the quiet on the isolated Carcass Island, far away from Stanley, as if it were "big city life," yet only a block long! When we had stopped for lunch in Stanley the day before, it seemed pretty quiet to me, even with some 75 tourists in the area.

Rockhopper Penguin Colony

We returned to the ship for lunch while we sailed to Westpoint Island, a short distance south. All of us birders looked forward to observing the Rockhopper Penguin colony located on the far side of the island.

Our Zodiac dropped us off on the shore and we headed to another remote sheep farm for afternoon tea, this time with Roddy and Lily Napier. The Napier family first established a farm on the island in 1860 and their descendants have owned the island ever since. When we arrived, Roddy amiably posed for photos next to a table loaded with sweet biscuits and candies.

After a brief visit, Roddy offered the option of an island tour with him in his Land Rover. The island was only five square miles so the tour fit our limited time schedule. A small group of our shipmates took him up on his offer. We birders were glad that most of the other passengers seemed content to wander along the beaches while we walked a little more than a mile to see the penguins. I carried my red jacket most of the way since it was too warm to wear. When we went ashore earlier that day I wore my jacket and my heavy fleece like a true explorer. Before long, I became overheated and almost fainted. The crew must have had a good laugh at our naiveté since most of the other people wore their red jackets, just like I had.

On the west side of the island near a rocky outcropping called the Devil's Nose, my friend Sally and I peeked over the edge of a cliff that plunged a long way down to the sea. A stiff wind whipped my hair into my eyes as I firmly planted my forward foot for safety and cautiously looked over the cliff for a better view. Small black-and-white spots below me streamed up and down the rocky slope. Simon, one of the naturalists from the ship, told us those were the rockhoppers. He pointed to a small clearing nearby and suggested we wait in the head-high tussock grass for a close-up look at the penguins.

The wind cooled us quickly in spite of the balmy air temperature so Sally and I joined the other birders, tucked out of the wind. While we waited, masses of rockhopper penguins and Black-browed Albatrosses entertained us with their activities about 50-feet away on the cliff face and to the right of a little meadow. Both species brayed to the universe, heads pointed at the sky, greeting their mates returning from the sea. The sounds melded into one loud, overwhelming cacophony, though later I learned to identify individual calls and gestures that the birds made.

The black-browed albatrosses had a white body and black wings when they were folded, with a faint black stripe flowing back from the eye like an eyebrow. Each pair had built a little pile of mud with a depression on top for an egg, but we were too early to see any of their eggs.

The rockhoppers prepared for breeding by moving around the small rocks that formed the nests. We learned more about those mobile rocks later in the trip. The penguins stood about two feet high and weighed around six pounds, had red eyes, a short, reddish-brown bill, and pink feet. A crest of starched feathers crowned the back of a rockhopper's head like a crew cut. On either side, a rakish swish of bright yellow feathers cast back from above each eye to a fetching droop that fluttered as the wind caught them. Sally gave a raucous cackle, then quipped, "They look like a bunch of punk rockers on their way to a Halloween party."

I agreed. They were such delightful creatures.

While rockhoppers can walk on flat land, they spend much of their time jumping up or down the steep rocky cliffs where they make their homes. They can hop up a rock face about half their own height from a standing start. It helps that they have strong claws and sandpaper feet to grip the rocky surfaces. On rocks close to us, we saw them jump down, sometimes further than the length of their little bodies.

A parade of rockhoppers ducked into the labyrinth of protective tunnels they had made at the base of the waving grass. Fifteen feet in front of our windbreak we could see an exposed ten-foot section of the penguin path. Even before the first penguins waddled into view, we could hear their noisy braying and chattering. By the time the penguins arrived at this stretch of the path, they had hopped and plodded their way up the entire 500-foot cliff.

The lead penguin spied us and stopped to study the gap in the grass. She turned back for a moment, uncertain, then forged ahead sensing no threat. The group of about ten penguins continued their march, single file, toward their nests further up the cliff.

Close up the rockhoppers reminded me of my two-year-old niece while she learned the finer points of moving forward. She pulled her arms back, thrust her chin forward, and toddled down the sidewalk slightly off balance. However, my niece could not hop up half her body height on the side of a cliff!

Simon answered our whispered questions as we waited. It seemed to me that the rockhoppers worked very hard to get up the cliffs, so I asked, "Why do they nest here? It's so difficult to get up that cliff."

"They always nest near steep rock gullies next to deep water," Simon explained. "It is their niche in the penguin world."

That made sense. Magellanic and gentoo penguins, both species bigger than the little rockhoppers, populated the sloping sandy beaches we had visited on Carcass Island. It may have been a matter of survival for the rockhoppers to develop an affinity for the deeper offshore waters.

Penguin bodies are built to swim. Their tough wings evolved to speed them toward food in the water and away from predators. Their short legs stream behind them when they swim and their feet work as rudders.

However, on land penguins must deal with gravity and a body not well designed for upright mobility. Penguin thighbones are short and fixed at the hip socket, so when they stand and walk upright the bones are relatively parallel to the ground. Imagine your thighs fused at a right angle. You have to squat and tilt forward to get your center of gravity over your feet. In addition, drape a lot of flesh between your ankles and try to walk. No wonder penguins look awkward.

A Last Look at the Rockhoppers

After leaving Westpoint Island, the ship sailed around the southern tip of land and into the bay where we observed with our binoculars the rockhoppers as they climbed from the bottom of the cliff up to their nests and back down again. From the aft deck of the ship, we could see the faint trail made by centuries of penguin toenail scratches winding up into the crown of grass. I watched one little rockhopper as she moved up the trail. She thrust her beak at an intended next step, maybe to examine the spot before leaping. She pulled back her flippers to balance against falling forward. Then, she took a hop that looked easy followed by her strong claws grabbing the new rock with amazing sureness. Half way up, the climb got tiresome for her. She pulled aside at a curve and flopped down on her fish-filled belly for a bit of a rest, then onward and upward.

We saw three species of penguins in the Falkland Islands; rockhoppers, Magellanic, and gentoos. I wondered how many more we might see in Antarctica.

With a last look at West Island, we retired to the dining room for the Captain's dinner. He officially welcomed us aboard and introduced the crew, many of whom we had informally met already.

At last, we were on our way to Antarctica!

Sir Ernest Shackleton's icebound ship Endurance

CHAPTER 3

Crossing Drake Passage

My fellow birders and I settled into life at sea, bound for Antarctica. Ahead of us lay Drake Passage, one of the most formidable and dangerous bodies of water known for the worst storms on earth and at times, icebergs. This tempestuous passage is located between Tierra del Fuego, Argentina and The Falkland Islands to the north, and the Antarctic Peninsula to the south.

I had reserved a cabin in the deepest part of the ship, which I figured would be the steadiest if the seas were rough. I based this decision on my sailing experience years earlier with my former husband on our 25-foot sailboat, and then our 65-foot schooner. We had experiences in rough seas on both boats, so I had firsthand knowledge on where to ride out violent storms in relative comfort. Lucky for me, the forecast predicted unusually mild weather for our passage so I anticipated a pleasant cruise to Antarctica.

Geographers named Drake Passage after the English explorer Sir Francis Drake. However, some Spanish and Latin American historians call this same passage *Mar de Hoces* after Spain's explorer,

Francisco Hoces, whom South American historians credit with discovering this passage some 75 years before Drake.

For years, this stretch of open water challenged sailing ships struggling to sail east or west against raging winds and tumultuous seas. Many ships sank with all hands aboard. Accounts written by explorers and shipping merchants who navigated these waters in square-rigged sailing ships, include horror stories about their struggles to get around the southern tip of South America and through Drake Passage. In one story, a ship made it around what sailors called "the Horn," but unfriendly winds blew the ship all the way back to where it had started.

The potentially fierce challenges of Drake Passage caused many captains to take their chances sailing among the islands at the southern tip of South America, trading the danger of high seas for that of fluky winds. It wasn't until the Panama Canal opened in 1914, connecting the Atlantic and Pacific Oceans, that trading ships could avoid the treacherous seas of Cape Horn and Drake Passage.

Shipboard Birding

Our first crossing of Drake Passage did end up being a pleasant and uneventful journey. The captain steered for the Antarctic Peninsula, the furthest point north of the Antarctic continent, while we spent hours on the sunny stern deck blissfully watching a cloud of sea birds drifting behind the ship. We did not need our binoculars since the birds hovered so closely. I listened eagerly while the more experienced birders easily identified the plethora of birds; Grey-headed Albatross, Southern Giant Petrels, Cape Petrels, Antarctic Prion, Sooty Shearwaters, Wilson's Petrels, and Grey-backed Storm-petrels. Dozens of birds soared astern, arriving and departing, dropping back, and then rushing up to the side of the ship again. The birders called out names so fast at times I only hoped I could remember a few of them.

In spite of the sun, the wind chilled me after about an hour, so I retreated to the lounge to warm up with a hot drink—at least until someone ducked in the door to announce the arrival of a new species. Then I rushed back outside to enjoy another new bird. With an average noon temperature of 43°F, including one high of 52°F, even some of the crew appeared on deck with their cameras and broad smiles.

Eight expedition staff members made themselves available to us on deck, and later on shore to answer our endless questions. Each one shared his expertise and personal stories during the lectures in the lounge. These inspiring talks accompanied by amazing photos fueled my excitement for our impending adventures. At the beginning of each lecture, Julio, the leader of the expedition staff and all our activities, introduced the speakers by listing their impressive and lengthy credits and years of experience in their respective fields. At one point, I wondered, *With all they do, why do they want to come on this tame trip with us?*

I soon realized that for at least some of them, this was a vacation. They had to give a lecture or two on topics they love, answer our questions, and then they got to hang out with fellow Antarctic experts. Fabulous!

Antarctic Convergence

Of course, we birders all attended the talk on "Birds of the South Atlantic" by Simon Cook, a well-known ornithologist who has traveled the world identifying and photographing birds as well as leading birding tours. We knew we would see only a limited number of species relative to birding locations in other parts of the world, but there would be birds in Antarctica that we would find in astonishing numbers, in itself a rarity for many birders. I looked forward to seeing many new species since I had done so little traveling. Almost every bird would be new to me since I was a rank beginner. While Simon talked, I imagined beaches full of nesting penguins awaiting us, along with clouds of terns, prions, and gulls.

A member of the expedition staff, geologist David Dallmeyer, Ph.D., gave a fascinating lecture on what is called the Antarctic Convergence. It is not an easy concept so I rely on the report given to us at the end of our voyage for the explanation.

The Antarctic Convergence is a line undulating between 50 and 60 degrees south running right around the continent, and well defined by water temperature readings. It is sometimes marked by a belt of fog or mist where warm, more saline currents coming south from the tropics meet cold, denser less saline currents moving north from Antarctica. These conflicting currents clash, converge and sink. The mixing waters provide a sympathetic environment for abundant plankton that nourish huge numbers of sea birds and mammals. However, few organisms cross this radical boundary, so it defines Antarctica physically and ecologically.

The Convergence is a zone about 20 to 30 miles wide, so when our ship entered the belt where the Convergence might occur, a crewmember kept an eye on the seawater temperature gauge to note the time when the temperature changed. On day four of the tour, about half way to the Antarctic continent and still in Drake Passage, the water temperature plunged from 52°F to 32°F and stayed there. This dramatic temperature drop indicated our ship had crossed the Antarctic Convergence.

The day before, the crew had organized a contest among the ship's passengers to predict what time we would cross the Antarctic Convergence. I had signed one of the empty lines on the scorecard without much thought. After we crossed the Convergence, I was in my cabin when Julio called my name over the speaker announcing that my guess was the closest. I won! My name appeared in the ship's daily newsletter and at the next gathering in the lounge, Julio presented me with a small, spiral-bound book containing chapters assembled by the expedition staff on everything a curious tourist might want to know about Antarctica. The tiny gift shop carried the book but mine was special—a prize. At that point in the tour, I felt stuffed with information from the lectures and all our activities, so I put the book in a drawer for later.

There were times after returning home when I wished I had paid more attention to the introductions and lectures and taken a few notes, but I told myself, *I'm on vacation. Taking notes would be too much like school.*

Luckily, I not only had my little book for reference, but at the end of the cruise we all received a 24-page summary of our trip that included black and white photos. Both of these resources have been valuable over the years as I've talked about my Antarctic experiences, and now, as I write about it.

After lunch on our second day at sea, Thanksgiving Day back home, the captain announced that we were approaching the tip of the Antarctic Peninsula. I became jittery with excitement. So close!

The captain ordered the ship's watertight doors to be closed for safety reasons, primarily from the threat of icebergs. I soon discovered a closed door next to my cabin that I hadn't noticed earlier. Since my cabin was on the lower deck, once the crew closed that door I had to take a longer route to the public areas on the main deck. That night, the intermittent clanging from below told me of a corresponding door the engine crew used. Whenever the crew changed shifts a great metallic crashing and electronic beeping accompanied each crewmember opening and shutting the door. Although annoying, I felt secure that if we hit an iceberg, we would not sink. However, I must admit that images of the great rip down the side of the Titanic did come to mind. I also realized safety clearly did not imply a good night's sleep.

Drawn by birds and the mysterious continent, I looked forward to experiencing the deafening brays of a thousand penguins, the sparkle of icebergs, the sting of ice-chilled air, and the startling blue sky in a place few have visited.

Right before Thanksgiving dinner, we spotted the rugged cliffs of Elephant Island, 582 miles south of the Falkland Islands and 152 miles north of the mainland of Antarctica.

Shackleton's Fateful Expedition

We enjoyed the mild, sunny weather that day while gazing at the rugged cliffs of Elephant Island thick with snow. Heavy clouds hung around the lofty peaks giving the island an ominous icy presence. The captain brought us as close as possible to the island while avoiding our first icebergs—thick slabs, sharp edged chunks, and softer rounded icebergs—all with the potential to do damage to our small polar ship.

Immediately, I thought about Shackleton's Imperial Trans-Antarctic Expedition 1914 to 1916 and all they endured in Antarctica. The sight of the towering peaks of Elephant Island had cheered the stranded Shackleton crew a year and a half after leaving South Georgia Island for the Antarctic. During that time, all had gone well until their ship, *Endurance*, became frozen in place on January 18, 1915, about 100 miles—one day's sail—from their destination. Ice held *Endurance* fast for 281 days while the ship drifted at least one thousand miles. The pressure of the ice on the ship's hull slowly increased. The men unloaded their supplies from the trapped ship along with the sled dogs, and on November 21, 1915, they watched as their crushed ship sank into the sea.

After the demise of *Endurance*, the crew had to pull loaded auxiliary boats across rough and shifting ice to open water. They sailed their small boats with the prevailing winds to Elephant Island where they found relief from the treacherous ice floes. With no rescue possible, Shackleton and five men sailed and rowed a 22-foot boat across 800 miles of the tempestuous southern Atlantic to South Georgia Island to get help. The rest of the crew waited four more months on Elephant Island for a ship to finally reach them. The waiting men experienced wretched weather like the men in the boats, but they were able to construct a crude shelter. They supplemented their dwindling food supply with penguin and seal meat cooked on blubber-fueled stoves. Melted glacial ice provided fresh water as long as the blubber-fuel held out.

I stood on the deck of our modern, comfortable ship and studied Cape Valentine where Shackleton and his crew made their first landing. The rough sea prevented us from landing on Elephant Island. I thought, *How relieved they must have been to find safe landing on solid ground after so many days living on dangerously deteriorating ice.*

A deep breath of polar air helped me to settle my profound awe for these men who survived four months in such a bleak place; and for the six who left that marginal security and launched their small boat in these massive uncertain waters. I had just crossed the southern Atlantic aboard the comfortable *Clipper Adventurer*, braced for the possibility of fierce storms and towering waves, which luckily never showed up. I marveled at the determination and courage that Shackleton and his crewmen mustered to once again brave the high seas in their small boat, believing they could find a distant island, South Georgia Island, and get help for the rest of the crew that waited on Elephant Island.

Our ship's log recorded a noon air temperature that day of 52°F. That would soon change.

Map of landing sites and our route around the

ANTARCTIC PENINSULA
and ISLANDS

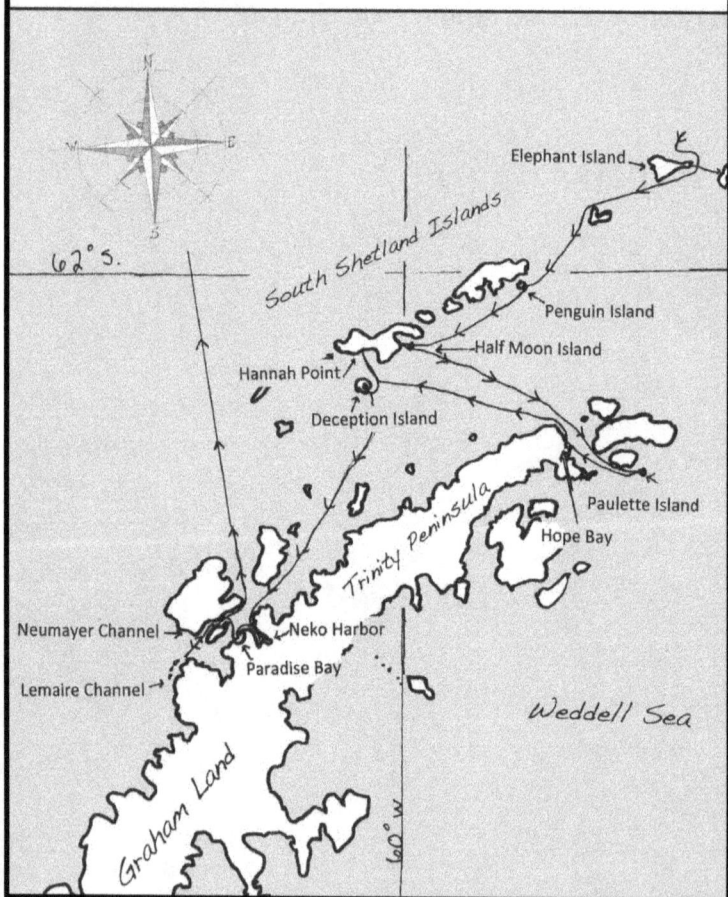

N
W E
S

62°S.

South Shetland Islands

Elephant Island

Penguin Island

Half Moon Island

Hannah Point

Deception Island

Paulette Island

Hope Bay

Trinity Peninsula

Neumayer Channel

Neko Harbor

Paradise Bay

Lemaire Channel

Weddell Sea

Graham Land

60°W

CHAPTER 4

A Foothold on Antarctica

After our tasty Thanksgiving dinner, we moved to the comfortable lounge where Julio prepared us, once again, for shore visits. The small craft landings in the Falkland Islands were practice runs—trials for proper clothing, transportation, and discipline. The mild consequences of mistakes during the Falkland shore landings were minimal. Now, anyone who wandered off in Antarctica could die. We listened carefully.

"Tomorrow, we will land on the rocky beach of Penguin Island, one of the South Shetland Islands. This is a 335-mile-long chain of islands located about 75 miles north of the Antarctic Peninsula." Julio pointed to his map on the wall. Then he added, "Several of our landing sites are in these islands because they are the first places to be free of snow and because of that, many of the research and whalers' stations are here.

"OK. This is your first test. Do you remember your landing group number?"

Everyone chuckled and repeated their number. He reminded us to remain in our cabins until he called our group for loading. "Finally, and most important, please do not forget to walk through the shallow pan of disinfectant on the departure deck to prevent passing disease from one colony to another. Do this coming and going. We must be very careful about this."

We all wore rubber boots from then on since any hikes were short. Each of us had to give our boots a swish for a few seconds in the unavoidable pan every time we passed through the departure deck, a crowded hall one deck above the water level where a large door could be opened to the outside. "Please remember that my crew can get anyone ashore who wants to go."

This was a generous offer because we had several passengers with mobility issues. I liked that he included everyone. I thought, *I could be one of those less able people at some time in the future. Who knows? Maybe this trip will be so fabulous I'll have to do it again!*

I was so excited I could hardly focus on what he said. My thoughts raced. *I know all that. Just get me into that Zodiac. I want to put my foot on Antarctica.*

That night I hardly slept. At last, the first light of day peeked through my porthole. *Oh, boy! Today I'll actually step where explorers walked almost one hundred years ago.*

At Last! Landing on Antarctica

Breakfast took forever. My group would be third to leave, so I partially dressed in long underwear, warm pants, waterproof rain pants, and overshoes. This time I needed every layer I had, but I held off putting on my fleece sweater and red jacket until the announcement for us to go to the landing area. My pack held my camera, binoculars, hat, gloves, and water, as instructed. The announcer made final suggestions on what to wear. "Be prepared for wind and sun. Don't forget your gloves."

I waited in my cabin as directed until the call for departures came over the cabin speaker. A woman's voice said, "Julio has gone ashore and found a site clear of wildlife for your landing and the shore crew is awaiting your arrival."

In the brisk air of Deck 2 I finished dressing, donned my life jacket, and cinched it up. Ready. A young crewman offered his strong hands as I climbed down the metal stairs to the floating Zodiac platform. Another crewmember helped me over the thick rubber sides of the inflatable boat and off we went. *Antarctica, here I come!*

The Zodiac bounced over small, choppy waves licked up by the stiff breeze. I was dressed for the harsh weather and grateful for all my heavy clothing. The ship's log reported a noon temperature of 38°F. *Spring weather! Think of that.*

Under overcast skies, I slid off the side of the Zodiac and waded the few steps to the pebbled shore peppered with occasional boulders. That was it. Suddenly, I was standing on Antarctica. *Ta Da!* Then I thought, *Where are the trumpets? The gongs? The cymbals?*

Mixing with the Local Wildlife

A nine-foot-long Weddell Seal raised a lazy eyelid to watch us pile up our lifejackets on the shore once we got off the Zodiacs. Abundant and placid, these seals are the most studied in Antarctica. Small Chinstrap Penguins nonchalantly walked past us, not far from the resting Weddell seals, uninterested in our activities. Chinstraps are one of the smallest penguins at 30 inches tall, distinguished by a white face with a black "strap" that goes under their chin. Several chinstrap penguins stood where a flow of small boulders tumbled into the sea. They studied the waves, waiting for the right one to arrive before plunging into the cold water.

Some passengers stayed on the beach to study the Elephant Seals, also known as sea elephants, with their fat floppy bodies as big as a legless elephant. A full grown male can weigh over 8,000 pounds, dive to 5,000 feet for food, and can be very aggressive during breeding season. These males have a giant proboscis (nose), like an elephant, the source of the species' name. Down the beach from us a jelly-wiggling heap of about ten of these seals seemed to be resting, eyes closed, after a good meal. I pitied the ones on the bottom of the pile. Not a giant nose among them, so we were safe.

After two days confined to the ship, I welcomed the optional climb up the edge of a volcanic cinder cone. Many of the islands in the Antarctic Peninsula are the remainders of volcanic activity, some fairly recent. Julio had promised us the opportunity to take advantage of one of nature's open-air spas at another stop, which I found intriguing. *What next?*

From the top of the cinder cone, we could see big and small ice chunks that filled the sea surrounding Penguin Island. Nearby King George Island looked like another old volcano. I marveled, *What a concept! There are volcanoes in Antarctica—as hard to believe as the glacier I saw years ago on Mount. Kilimanjaro located right on the equator. This Earth is so amazing.*

Back on the gravelly beach, I strolled past bleached whalebones, bits of wood, and streams of chinstrap penguins marching to and from the ocean to their colony on the steep slope behind the beach. The loud penguin calls increased in volume and filled the air as we approached the colony. The Giant Petrels nesting up the hill behind the chinstraps flew in and out with food for their chicks. We stayed a good distance from the nests so we didn't disturb them since we noticed skuas, a group of seabirds, watching for unattended eggs.

Julio was the beach master that day, so we peppered him with questions. I needed confirmation that we were *actually* on Antarctica's land mass.

"Yes, this is Antarctica, but it is not the mainland. We are saving that for another landing."

OK, I wasn't on the mainland of Antarctica, but technically we were on Penguin Island, which was good enough for me. And for the many tourists on the huge ships, they only got a view of these islands—no shore trips at all. I was excited that we would have many more opportunities to go ashore before the end of this trip! Yay!

For a moment, I stopped and slowly looked around. I mused, *How do I freeze this moment in my mind—this sensation of physically being here? Just breathe it in. Just breathe it in.*

We had about two hours to sit, climb, and explore the island. After that, we all made it back to the Zodiacs at the appointed time.

Half Moon Island & the Lonely Dinghy

On our way to the next stop, several Antarctic Petrels with their bold, brown-and-white markings, flew in synchronized formation behind the ship as others had on our way south. In the afternoon, the sun broke through but the wind still felt sharp.

On Half Moon Island we had another chance to see wildlife and remnants of human history on the shore. Right away, the partially decayed, open wooden boat, 25-feet long and half covered with snow, grabbed my interest. Julio thought the beamy and heavily built boat could have been a water tender to a whaling ship. The boat had been built using lapstrake construction, a method of attaching planks to frames and to themselves that added strength to the hull. This reminded me of my own sailing days when I lived in Port Townsend, Washington. The town is a center for wooden boat building and a few artisans there continue to build wooden dinghies using lapstrake construction.

That sturdy dinghy on the shore of Half Moon Island must have been there for at least 75 years. In Oregon, it would have been totally rotted with ferns growing out of it, but in the cold of Antarctica the well-built craft held together amazingly well. Later, I realized that the old tender was about the size of boat that Shackleton and his men sailed and rowed on their

800-mile, epic journey from Elephant Island to South Georgia Island. My former husband and I had sailed a fiberglass boat about the same size from San Diego to Mazatlan, and back. As we sailed north toward San Diego, the November winds gusted to 40 knots, which the Beaufort wind force scale describes as "gale force." Shackleton and his crew had to battle far worse weather and in an open boat.

After studying the boat for a long time, I looked up and noticed a chinstrap penguin struggling through mushy snow from her nest up the hill. The half-melted snow did not allow her to march with confidence and she often broke through a patch of crusty ice. Half snowbound, she had the choice to work hard to regain her upright posture or she could slide on her belly, pushing with her feet on the mushy snow. She alternated between the two modes of travel, taking much longer than it would have taken traversing hard snow or clean rocks. This penguin must have been exhausted, but I doubt she worried about it. Driven by instinct, wild animals just do what needs to be done.

Harriet and a tabular iceberg in Iceberg Alley.

CHAPTER 5

My First Steps on the Continent

At six in the morning of the sixth day, I awoke to Julio's low voice over the speaker in my room. He almost whispered, "If you are awake, come up on deck to see the icebergs."

Jumping into my clothes, I donned my red jacket, and hurried up the two flights of stairs. Through sleepy eyes, I watched in awe as we passed massive tabular icebergs with flat tops and straight sides so large they dwarfed our ship. All of us early birds stood on the deck mesmerized by the beauty and size of the icebergs. The stunning colors ranged from deep blue and blue-green to a lighter blue to the most predominant white, depending on how much air the ice contained. The ship inched along with just enough movement to steer so we could take a long look without hitting an iceberg. We had entered Iceberg Alley, a name well earned. Wind and currents conspire to keep Iceberg Alley, also known as Antarctic Sound, reliably full of tabular icebergs floating freely in the water, their sparkling bulk several times the size of our 330-foot vessel.

Without something for size comparison, I asked Julio, "How tall are these icebergs?"

"Well, these are not really big ones, maybe one hundred feet high, about as tall as a ten-story building. And remember, only ten percent of the berg by weight is above water. These all go way down."

"So, what's a really big one?" I asked.

"Oh, I think the largest one reported was close to the size of Connecticut. It floated around for about three years. They even tracked it by satellite."

So, these bergs are the pipsqueaks, I thought. *Oh, my.*

Julio added, "We'll see a lot of the smaller ones, the bergy bits, that are up to sixteen feet high, and growlers, smaller than three feet."

Icebergs originate on land as glacier ice. The weight of years of snowfall on the glaciers compresses any air trapped in the ice below, making the ice very dense. Put this ice in water and it fizzes as the air expands. All glacier ice behaves like this. I first saw this phenomenon as a teenager at a science exhibit in 1962 at the Seattle World's Fair. An Inuit in native clothing at the Alaskan tourism booth showed this glacier activity to visitors. I found the demonstration so interesting that I watched it three times.

A glacier in Antarctica and Alaska takes millennia to slide across the rock base and slip into the bay, thus, our expression "at glacial speed" for "really slow." Once free of the land, and with only seawater under the compacted and floating ice sheet, the glacier fractures and eventually breaks up, and the pieces float off in the form of the tabular icebergs we saw in Iceberg Alley. After wind and sea work on the shapes of these enormous chunks of ice, they can be extremely dangerous. They lose bulk below the water, become unstable, and can suddenly turn over without warning, reorienting to the new distribution of mass. I wondered if anyone has ever seen an iceberg flip over, something I would love to see.

This reminded me of a similar quick and rarely seen event that I had witnessed: a tree falling in the forest. It occurred on the shore of the Amazon River in a tropical Peruvian jungle. A rifle-crack-like sound from the snap of the critical vine holding up a heavy tree announced the beginning. A small group of us watched as the tree slowly broke away from the others, accompanied by loud cracks and pops as the vines that climbed the trunk broke. Tangled in a web of other vines and trees, the tree fell to the forest floor. It would be hard for any tour company to schedule such an event and we were delighted at the surprise!

Our ship sailed 30 miles through Iceberg Alley, the 7-to-10-mile-wide passage between the tip of the Trinity Peninsula, the northern most point of continental Antarctica, and several of the many offshore islands.

Esperanza Base

I ate breakfast in the ship's warm dining room and enjoyed watching the icebergs as we slowly navigated to the east end of Iceberg Alley and anchored in Hope Bay. A small cluster of buildings perched on the edge of the continent in this small bay. Their corrugated metal roofs and red painted sides were characteristic of most of the aging buildings we saw in Antarctica.

This Argentine settlement, called Esperanza Base, was built in 1952. (*Esperanza* is the Spanish word for hope.) The Argentines maintain the handful of buildings year round with only a small staff remaining during the winter.

The previous evening's lecture prepared us for this extraordinary opportunity to set foot on Antarctica, the continent itself, rather than just one of the islands. We knew the rules: No souvenirs and don't remove feathers, rocks, sand—*anything*. Imagine the impact if thousands of tourists each took a handful of penguin stones.

Hawaiians protect Haleakala, one of their sacred volcanoes, by telling tourists they will have bad luck if they take *anything* from there. It works for them. Maybe the Antarctic operators need to start a similar myth, especially since the association of tour operators in Antarctica are invested in keeping the continent appealing to their clients. Unfortunately for me, I had planned to collect penguin stones as my gifts for friends and family. Immediately, I had to reconsider my options and respect the high value the penguins placed on each precious stone.

After a brief ride in the Zodiac, we arrived at the landing site, a sloping gravel beach near the buildings. When I climbed out of the boat, I had that same thrill as when I stepped on to Penguin Island, but this time I stepped on to the *continent* of Antarctica for the first time. *Wow,* I thought, *if could just keep walking, I could be at the South Pole in no time. Very funny, Harriet!*

I moved away from the rest of the group to spend a little time alone. Taking a deep breath, I savored the moment. I closed my eyes and listened to the *shush* of the waves, the murmur of the other passengers in the distance, and distant penguin calls. I gazed at the rippling water and in the distance, steep rocky crags starkly jutting out of the ocean. I breathed it all in—Antarctica. *I am standing on Antarctica.* That astounding realization melted into my body.

After several minutes I pulled myself away to join the others for a brief tour of the settlement. A young Argentine man offered to show us his home. Tinny music, thin and metallic, blared over old loudspeakers, following us from the outside to the inside during our tour. It was annoying to say the least, but maybe the quiet that I loved became too much for the residents after months and months of it. The station included a school for the staff's 20 or so kids. The students must have been at lunch when we peeked into the simple schoolroom and only saw a chalkboard. We also visited a small one-room museum and a commissary where we could send a postcard with Esperanza Base's unique postal stamp. I sent a card to myself as a reminder of my visit to this wonderful place. That ended our brief tour of the buildings, so our guide proudly suggested we visit the Adélie Penguin colony behind the base.

The early French explorer, Dumont d'Urville, named the Adélie penguins after his wife. They are one of the smallest penguins and have a stark white front, a pitch-black head and back, and a white ring around each eye. Years before my visit, I read that not only had the Esperanza Base been built on top of the largest Adélie penguin nesting colony in the world, but that trash from the base encroached upon what remained of the colony. Although Antarctica had called to me most of my life, I did not want to participate in the destruction of such a treasure. Then things changed. In the late 1980s, research stations began to recognize the damage they were doing to the environment, especially with the dumping of toxic wastes. By 2001, the colony had 125,000 nesting pairs and one staff person at the base whose sole duty is to protect the penguins and their surrounding environment. When we visited, the penguin protector had roped off the colony to prevent trespassing after the penguins leave for their post-breeding migrations.

One pair of Adélies_had already laid their two eggs. The brooding bird lay flat on the nest while the others busily moved rocks from one place to another. Choosing the right pebble seemed to take great concentration, but as I watched the penguins' activities a helicopter flew off from the base, completely destroying my mood. After a short period of frantic activity, the Adélies settled down again. I noted that the penguin on the nest had stayed glued to her spot, adding to the frustration of the hovering skuas looking for a meal.

Finding a Souvenir

Fortunately, I did discover an exception to the no-souvenir rule. While we waited for our Zodiac ride back to the ship from Esperanza Base, I spotted a large building where the staff sorted trash for appropriate disposal. I asked the ship's shore captain who waited with us, "Is there still a problem with the base being built on the Adélie colony?"

"Oh, a little. The Argentines removed their trash after the nations involved in research in Antarctica signed the agreement in 1959 to clean up the sites," explained the guide. "But there is still small stuff in the rocks behind the sorting building."

"Would anyone mind if I took some of the bits home?" I asked.

His face lit up at the novel idea. "The tour operators' association might even make you a member if you did," he chuckled.

Not waiting for him to retract his invitation, I sauntered over to the rock-filled pier where the rusty metal clutter lay tucked among the small round rocks. I pretended to study the few nests and birds nearby in case someone should see me. With my boot, I scuffled the stones, unearthing the bent nails, washers, brittle cable pieces, and my prize, two angle irons held together with a large bolt. *This could be a new activity for tourists,* I thought. *Trash removal. Bring home a genuine piece of Antarctica trash.*

I stuffed my treasures in my pockets—I had big pockets—and strolled back to the landing pier. Spotting a stone hut down the beach a way, I asked Julio about it.

"Three members of the Swedish Antarctic Expedition spent a terrible winter in that hut in 1903," Julio explained. "The base staff rebuilt it recently to honor the hardships endured by those three explorers."

That accounted for the hut's good condition. My Zodiac arrived, and I forgot about the hut—that is until we visited Paulet Island, which played a role in the Shackleton saga.

*The restored stone hut at Esperanza station, typical of emergency shelters
built by stranded sailors and explorers for survival until rescue.*

CHAPTER 6

Crossing Paths
of the Explorers

Our ship continued southeast through Antarctic Sound, the official name of Iceberg Alley. Our destination, Paulet Island, had an interesting history and one of the largest Adélie penguin colonies in the world. The breakers were so strong when we approached the shore of Paulet Island, the crew had to tie the stern of our Zodiac to a rock so the bow faced the rough waves that could swamp it. The brisk wind whipped our sturdy jackets and a weak sun fooled us into thinking it might be warmer than the 38°F.

Walking down the beach away from the others, I took a deep breath and twitched to feel my body. *Yes, I am here. This is real— so much history on this island.*

At first, I followed the others down the shingle beach of small-to-medium-sized pebbles. It made walking a challenge as we made our way along the shore toward the closest Adélie colony.

Most tourists who visit Paulet Island come to see the more than 100,000 pairs of penguins that populate the circular island, which is less than a mile across. The colony covered most of the island, so it wasn't hard to find. I watched with the others for a while, but Paulet Island rang in my head as an important link to the Shackleton saga. I wanted to see the hut Shackleton had tried to reach in order to save his men. It turns out that the hut in Hope Bay was also part of the ship *Antarctic's* story and how the hut on Paulet got built.

Before Shackleton

Otto Nordenskjold led the Swedish Antarctic Expedition to the Antarctic Peninsula from 1901 to 1904. During this exploratory journey, he named Antarctic Sound for his ship named *Antarctic,* the first vessel to navigate the full length of this body of water. At the beginning of the Antarctic winter of 1902, the northern hemisphere's summer, the ship sailed west to east through the Antarctic Sound, passed Paulet Island and turned south. The expedition dropped off five men including Nordenskjold, on Snowhill Island located south of Paulet Island in the Weddell Sea. The explorers spent the winter there and continued collecting data. By then, all the men were familiar with the Antarctic Sound region.

The ship sailed back through Antarctic Sound and turned north for the Falklands. Several months later, *Antarctic* returned to pick up the five men on Snow Hill Island. However, the weather stayed cold that Antarctic summer, much the same as the year Shackleton arrived. Captain Carl Larsen realized they might not be able to pick up Nordenskjold's party before winter set in again. Nordenskjold and Larsen, familiar with the vagaries of the Antarctic, had planned for this possibility and the ship had dropped three men at Hope Bay to construct a depot with supplies in case Nordenskjold's party had to spend another winter. They could be more mobile on land than the ship at sea and would know where the extra supplies would be dropped. The ship tried to reach them, but ironically, during that effort *Antarctic* sank in the Antarctic Sound about 25 miles off the coast of Paulet Island, short of Snowhill Island.

The crewmembers of *Antarctic* found refuge on Paulet Island. Here, the 20 crewmen built the small thick-walled stone hut, 34 feet by 22 feet, to protect them against the extreme cold. They also killed as many penguins as they could for food and fuel during the winter. Amazingly, when spring finally arrived, *Antarctic's* crew from Paulet Island and Nordenskjold's party of five from Snow Hill all joined the three men who wintered at Hope Bay. To give a sense of distances, Snow Hill Island is about 75 miles from both Hope Bay and Paulet Island, and those two islands are 40 miles apart.

Within days of their reunion at Hope Bay, and nine months after *Antarctic* sank, an Argentine ship, *Uruguay,* rescued them all as arranged in a fall-back plan should *Antarctic* not return. *Uruguay* left new supplies in the stone hut on Paulet Island for future stranded sailors. As fate would have it, Ernest Shackleton, while living in London, England at the time, purchased the supplies in 1903 on behalf of the

Argentine government and delivered by *Uruguay*. In 1915, Shackleton himself tried to reach this stone hut after pressure ice crushed his own ship, *Endurance*.

With a strong sense of this island's history with explorers, it felt surreal to be walking on Paulet Island—the very island where that stone hut had stood. I admit to some disappointment when I actually found the hut on a stony ridge above the Adélie colony. Recalling how Julio had described the *Antarctic* crew's chilling account of the rugged determination to survive, I gasped when I first saw the heaps of rock that outlined where the hut's walls had been. It all became very real as I studied the remnants. *These are the walls built by men almost one hundred years ago, just as Shackleton's men had done on Elephant Island.*

I found the mellow gurgle of the waves on the rocks relaxing as I mused about the crewmembers of *Antarctic* who lived in that small stone hut for so long, hoping to be rescued. I imagined what the hut must have looked like when it was in use. I had read that the stone hut's roof was made of sealskin, supported, I imagine, with wood from the small boat that brought them to the island. The men lived with the stench of uncured skins since it would have been impossible to properly cure them. The crew knew they could only heat the hut to freezing, or else risk melting the snow and ice chips they used to fill in between the rocks. Eventually, the skins became coated with rancid, greasy smoke from the blubber stove the men used. It must've been incredibly arduous surviving under those conditions, but it was their only choice. As sailors in those waters, they knew the risks and carried tools to survive.

There was nothing quite like standing in front of an ancient structure, regardless of its condition, used by men I felt I knew. Next to that crumbled stone hut I felt the vibrations of the men from *Antarctic* flow through me, as if my very presence evoked their ghosts. In my mind's eye, I almost expected a stooped figure to emerge from the door of the hut with long hair and beard and ragged clothing, smelling like rancid grease, rotting sealskins, and smoke.

Shackleton's Travails & Leadership

Shackleton's crew lived under the same conditions as the crew from *Antarctic,* surviving for many months despite brutal polar conditions. All of this made me wonder, *Why do men go exploring in these remote places when this can happen?*

What I had garnered from other books on explorers was that they were lured by the excitement of the adventure and the thrilling edge of taking enormous risks. Polar explorers returned to Antarctica again and again. I have always been intrigued with these kinds of expeditions; perhaps it's because I have a bit of that trait in myself. My trip to Antarctica was not exactly on the beaten path of tourism and I have always sought out the unusual and challenging trips.

Back aboard *Clipper Adventurer,* I leaned on the aft rail and mused about what motivates explorers. The captain reversed course, leaving Paulet Island behind us. Gazing past the little island, I studied the

65

sea beyond thick with icebergs and chunks of ice that rolled down past the horizon. So much of the Shackleton saga had occurred there on the waters and ice of the Weddell Sea. Lost in my thoughts, I reviewed some of the key events of Shackleton's travails beginning with, *How did he get into that awful situation in the first place?*

In 1915, Ernest Shackleton sailed *Endurance* from the South Georgia Islands southeast of the Falklands into the Weddell Sea, east of the Antarctic Peninsula. He intended to launch the Imperial Trans Arctic Expedition to cross the south polar continent. Powered by a 350-horsepower, coal-fired steam engine, *Endurance* chugged along in the narrow band of summer water between the remaining ice and the shore. However, fewer than 200 miles from their destination, unseasonable freezing winds locked the ship in ice on January 18, 1915, just one day's travel from their destination. When release from the ice seemed unlikely, the 28 men and 69 sled dogs settled in to wait out the long, coldest months on a ship loaded with food, fuel, and equipment.

On May 1, the sun disappeared for four months. The sun had almost returned on September 2 when the ice's pressure squeezed the hull of *Endurance* and, according to one crewman, it "jumped into the air to settle on its beam (side)." Pressure ice forms when thick, floating sheets of ice rub together, forcing small chunks into ridges and emitting eerie, haunting groans and squeals. Caught in this pressure ice, *Endurance* was doomed.

The men hauled supplies onto the ice and on October 27, Shackleton gave the order to abandon ship. The men camped nearby until the ship sank on November 21, ten months after becoming ice-bound. Frank Worsley, the captain and navigator of *Endurance,* kept track of their location as the polar winds and vicious weather pushed the men camped on the ice floes around the perimeter of the Weddell Sea. When the ship sank, the ice pack was moving in the direction of safety. Worsley and Shackleton knew they must reach either Paulet Island where supplies awaited them, or Elephant Island where rescue might be possible from ships carrying whalers or explorers.

They camped, hauling as they could, using up their food, eating some of the dogs, and hoping to reach open water. As the weather moderated and the ice became weaker, squeals from moving ice never let the men forget that at any moment a fissure on the ice floe could split the camp in two. The floes became smaller as the weather warmed and the danger increased.

Worsley calculated that the men were about 346 miles from Paulet Island where Shackleton had sent supplies several years before. However, still far from open water, Worsley determined that Paulet Island would be too difficult to reach given the direction of the moving ice pack. The men were only able to average one and a half miles a day hauling their three small loaded boats, pulled by the dogs and pushed by the men, so they had to take advantage of the motion of the ice as much as possible.

Shackleton had to change his destination further north to ice-covered and mountainous Elephant Island, a more realistic destination given the movement of the ice. It was April when the ice opened enough for the men to launch their boats. They shoved them into the open water that was still full of loose pack ice, and rowed and sailed through rough seas and high winds for nine horrendous days. Finally, they made it to Elephant Island on April 16, 1916, fifteen months after *Endurance* had first been frozen in place.

The three small boats landed at Valentine Point, the land we had seen after our ship rounded Elephant Island. Exhausted and relieved to be on solid ground, the men had to pack up again to find a more suitable camping spot. They rowed around the north side of Elephant Island to Cape Wild. It wasn't a great camp, but better than the first for a long-term camp.

Shackleton and Worsley made the difficult decision to take their best boat, the *James Caird,* to sail and row east, hoping to find South Georgia Island, 800 miles across the wild ocean. Shackleton thought this was their best chance to find help to rescue the remainder of the crew. Four of the fittest crewmen joined them to help row. They reached their destination because of the crewmen's sheer grit and stamina, along with Worsley's ability to navigate such a small boat on a raging sea.

When I read about Worsley's navigational skills, I was overwhelmed because I had a sense of how difficult it could be to navigate on the open sea. When I sailed from San Diego south to Cabo San Lucas, Mexico with my former husband in 1969 in our 25-foot sailboat, we used a sextant for navigation, the same type of instrument that Worsley used. Though anachronistic even in our time, that sextant was a beautiful tool but a challenge to use. We only needed navigation to help us know whether we were north or south of a protected bay to anchor for the night on the long stretch of the Baja California coast. Our lives were never in serious danger, unlike Shackleton's crew.

Worsley found South Georgia Island using his sextant—a target about ninety miles long—navigating across 800 miles of rough seas that, at times, had hurricane-force winds. In addition, Worsley had guided their deteriorating little boat to the deepest bay on Elephant Island, giving the three men who walked the thirty-two miles for help the best chance of success. They hiked for 36 hours without a break across the rocky, peak-covered island, a feat unmatched today. Had Worsley been less competent, all 28 men would have perished.

Imagining the Antarctic Explorers' Journeys

In addition to seeing Antarctic penguins and other birds, this trip brought to life my intense interest in the Shackleton expedition, as well as other notable expeditions to this rugged continent. I projected myself into the explorers' adventures and dangerous situations. I imagined the cold wind that tried to freeze them all and how hard they must have worked, day in and day out, often without adequate food.

Trying to put myself in their situations, I imagined the mental stress would have been my greatest challenge, not so much the physical challenges. But then, I don't think I would've been chosen for such a trip either.

On this trip, I witnessed firsthand a gentler form of those rugged conditions and it was no piece of cake. I must admit that when I returned to the ship after visiting Paulet Island, I was grateful to sit down with other passengers for a lovely lunch. *Thank heavens.*

Later, we would face far worse conditions, similar to those the explorers endured.

Harriet enjoying the Deception Island "spa" near Whalers Cove.
The ship is in the background.

CHAPTER 7

Penguins, and More Penguins

Leaving Paulet Island to the penguins, *Clipper Adventurer* retraced our route through Iceberg Alley during the night. The next morning, we early risers enjoyed a pod of Orcas leaping and spouting for several minutes in front of the ship's bow. And as quickly as they arrived, they were gone. What fun! As I watched them cavort, I thought of the same scene I enjoyed from my sailing days with dolphins playfully swimming and leaping near the bow of our sailboat. Two or three usually surfaced right next to the cockpit of our 25-foot boat, scaring me out of my peaceful thoughts with their loud exhalations. The powerful bow wave in front of *Clipper Adventurer* attracted more Orcas than our little sailboat had done.

We returned to the South Shetland Islands on our seventh day and Hannah Point on Livingstone Island, where we visited another chinstrap penguin colony. A stream of busy penguins trekked to and from the sea, weaving their way through the thousands of nests, risking the displeasure of the occupant of any nest if they got too close. The snow had melted so many penguin parents were brooding their one or two eggs. I sat and watched a small group from a distance.

Luckily, I got to witness a nearby penguin walk up to a nesting partner. They both stood chest to chest, twining and weaving their necks in recognition, braying a greeting—perhaps passing on news. Then, they switched places. The off-duty penguin stretched, stepped to the side of the nest, and began to preen, important for proper buoyancy. The other penguin positioned her feet on either side of the nest, and then poked and prodded the eggs to turn them. She waggled her brood patch, the warm, featherless skin on her lower belly, and placed it over the egg and settled down. She seemed to heave a sigh, ready for some rest after a morning at sea. Well, maybe it was my imagination that she sighed, but I would have if I had been in her place. What a gift to watch the changing of the breeder birds!

These penguins, like others, primarily survive on krill, the small shrimp-like crustaceans that live under ice shelves.

About ten years after my trip to Antarctica, the area's krill population had become threatened by a developing krill fishery (aquaculture) in the southern oceans of South America, as well as by overfishing and climate change. Recently discovered information that the pink krill oil might be a good antioxidant for aging bodies could be another nail in the coffin for this essential food source. If these human-influenced detriments continue to deplete the krill population, most of the creatures that live around the Antarctic Continent will be devastated.

Whaling Days & a Spa

Deception Island is actually the water-filled top of an active volcano that last erupted in 1967 and 1969, destroying two scientific stations inside the crater, but no lives were lost. We steamed around the hilly face of the circular island that protected its watery center. When we came to a small gap, the captain carefully navigated the ship through Neptune's Bellows, the entry channel less than 800 feet wide and framed by tall hills. One of the world's greatest and safest natural harbors opened before us. Thousand-foot-high cliffs surrounded the seven-mile-wide harbor within the volcano island's caldera. Heavy clouds obscured the top of the cliffs and heaps of old snow lingered in the shadows on the shore, giving the island a mysterious aura.

Whaler's Bay is tucked away in one of the many indentations on the inside of the caldera. On a flatter section of beach, whalers had built their whale-blubber processing station. Rusted remains of the crumbling metal rendering tanks from the nineteenth and twentieth century still stood, along with an old aircraft hangar constructed in more recent times for scientific studies. The commercial tanks felt incongruous after seeing so many places without manmade structures. No penguins wandered around as they had in other places, which surprised me. One of the guides explained that the fishing is better on the other side of the ridge where we passed the busy penguin colony at Baily Head on the eastern most extremity of the island before entering the harbor.

Hot water fed by underground volcanic activity seeped into nearby Pendulum Cove, near the whaling station. I don't know how many of the whalers took advantage of that Antarctic spa, but I eagerly joined the exotic adventurers on our trip, ready for another "first" event. Willing to try anything, a handful of us wore our swimsuits under warmer garb and climbed into the Zodiacs for our shore journey. As we had been instructed, we each dug out a shallow depression in the ankle deep water between the dry rocky beach and the rippling wavelets. I looked around at the others hard at work pulling rocks aside in their swimsuits here in Antarctic, and thought, *Is this absurd, or what?*

I turned back to my task. Steam rose from the gravel hinting at warmth, so I stripped off my coverings and plopped into three inches of tepid sea-water. Sitting in the warm pool, my legs and backside were warmish but the rest of me rapidly cooled in the 41°F air. I thought, *OK, what now?*

Meanwhile, the rest of the curious tourists had come ashore to gape at our amazing display. Two hearty Brits even swam in the cooler water beyond the band of heated pools but not me. As soon as Sally photographed my ridiculous predicament, I jumped up and raced for a towel.

Penguin Life

Over lunch we chatted with one of our nature staff about shore trips and penguins, of course. We all enjoyed the shore excursions, the opportunity to closely examine such a unique environment and get some exercise while breathing some of the purest air on earth. I liked the crunchy grinding sound that echoed in the hollow chambers of the Zodiac when we landed for day excursions. It reminded me of the many times I'd run ashore from our sailboat in Mexico, yet, here I was in Antarctica!

Though the staff chose landing sites carefully so our activity would not disturb the penguins, seals, and other wildlife, this did not stop the penguins from marching through our midst. We were allowed to wait to see if they might be curious about us; since we all had seen pictures of people and penguin interactions. Each of us hoped for our own personal encounter but few people had one. Personally, I felt the penguins found me as interesting as a rock.

The penguin colonies on the Antarctic Peninsula consist primarily of Adélies, gentoos, and chinstraps. All have the characteristic white front and black back, and for good reason. From below, a predator has difficulty seeing a white belly against the sky.

The mature male penguins are the first to return to the nesting grounds, even before the snow melts. Each male knows where his own pile of special stones is located. Soon after, the female arrives and together, they wait. Frequent spontaneous calls insure that their neighbors understand who owns that spot.

When a partner returns from dinner in the sea, they renew their bond with snaking necks and loud barking greetings shouted skyward.

The ample flesh under the belly of each parent is important for incubation because the naked brood pouch in the middle of the fold is rich in blood vessels, as with other birds. For example, when a mother penguin returns to the nest, she straddles the egg and adjusts her baggy lower regions around the orb so her brood pouch is properly positioned over the eggs for maximum warmth. When it's the father's turn, he does the same with his brood pouch. However, a penguin cannot preen while incubating. Preening must be carefully done for warmth and buoyancy in the icy water, so when the mother or father leaves the egg-sitting duty, she or he first takes time to revive the oil on their feathers.

Julio often reminded us to give the nesting penguins a wide berth because we could expose the nest to predation. Plus, if we got too close the defensive parent could give us a good whack. As flightless birds, penguins, like the steamer ducks, use their wings as weapons. One of the scientists who spent time in a penguin colony, banding chicks, verified how painful a good crack to the shin could be.

I enjoyed just watching the penguins go about their business. They marched up and down hills, stole the walnut-sized rocks from other nests, or greeted each other with snaking head bobs. Sometimes they called out with their hoarse, donkey-like braying. Other times, further south the penguins patiently waited for the snow to melt, the egg to be laid, or the chick to hatch. We encountered other birds as well. Large Brown Skuas and white, dove-like Snowy Sheathbills watched us closely for scavenging opportunities should we get too close to a penguin's nest and cause a parent to leave a chick or egg unattended.

Our December visit was too early for the most frantic portion of penguin parenting when the ravenous chicks exhaust the parents with their incessant demands. We only saw recent hatches in a few places, but photographs during the lectures aboard ship showed the chicks almost the size of their parents, covered with fine down, and with gaping, begging mouths. It's no wonder the parents leave altogether when the chicks have finished their molt in their preparation to depart. By that time, the frazzled moms and dads need to feed themselves after raising their chicks to self-sufficiency.

The adult penguins also need to molt and replace their feathers annually. After completing their parenting duties, exhausted parents head north to other feeding grounds. They find a good place to feed and regain their weight and prepare for their molt. Then they hitch a ride on a northbound iceberg, one of the smaller ones that has melted into an odd shape with a low side so the penguins can easily hop onto their chariot. Penguins without feathers are not buoyant and cannot go into the water until they are fully insulated again, so an iceberg offers safety and a relaxing boost to their journey. It takes about a month for all the new feathers to grow in again, displacing the old ones. This is called a "catastrophic molt" in contrast to most birds that molt a few feathers at a time.

When penguins are not nesting, they range widely in the Southern Hemisphere. In the southern spring after roaming the seas, some species, including the rockhoppers and Adélies, return to the Falklands or the Antarctic shores to set up house again. No penguins live north of the equator with the exception of a tiny population of endemic Galapagos Penguins. The two penguins I saw when visiting the Galapagos looked so lonesome compared to these huge Antarctic colonies. Only five-and-a-half pounds, the Galapagos Penguins survive in that tropical environment because the waters around the islands are so cold.

Crabeater Seals & Magical Silence

During the night, our ship steamed about 145 miles south and west from Deception Island, and south to the west side of the Antarctic Peninsula to visit two spectacular bays, Neko and Paradise Harbors. Located closer to the South Pole, the ship had to shoulder aside more and larger chunks of floating ice, and thicker snow covered the shore. The water temperature stayed a constant 32°F, while the air temperature fluctuated in the 40s.

Eight days into the trip, we enjoyed a different perspective. On a Zodiac tour of Paradise Harbor we got much closer to some of the wildlife. With only a light breeze and full sun, we basked in the awe-inspiring view of glaciated mountains with ice-covered slopes that plunged into the harbor.

We approached a six-foot-long Crabeater Seal, fat and content, sleeping soundly on a thick sheet of ice floating only a few inches above the surface of the water. The seal raised his head and opened a sleepy eye, surveying our craft and us. Luckily, we did not qualify as interesting, so he flopped his head down again. Crabeater seals never go ashore and only rest on convenient icebergs. They eat mostly krill, and in turn, young crabeater seals are the primary food for the Leopard Seals. Ultimately, everything depends on the krill.

Several hundred Adélie penguins wandered around the scattered red buildings of an unoccupied Chilean research station as we motored past. The Adélies waited for the snow to melt off their rock nests. Since penguins poop as needed, the snow looks dirty from a distance but it is really pink from the krill the penguins eat. Their numbers were not as great as the penguins at other colonies, and I wondered if the Chileans had someone to protect the Adélies when they occupied the station, as the Argentines did.

My Zodiac had been pressed into service to accommodate the last of the passengers wanting to go on the popular tour. The unusually loud and raspy motor assaulted my senses while surrounded by such pristine scenery. One friend who had visited the Antarctic Peninsula previously, had told me that she especially loved the utter silence. I longed for that experience, and finally asked the boat driver, "Can we have some time without the motor?"

Far from the ship and the other motoring Zodiacs, the driver obliged. We drifted quietly for a while, each of us lost in our own thoughts amidst the magnificence of Paradise Harbor, a serene delight. That deep silence can only be experienced away from wildlife, especially penguin colonies with their cacophony of calls, brays, and general penguin chatter. Even resting seals like the crabeater will grunt, burp, fart, and slap their floppy skin on the ice as they wiggle to change position while half asleep; a delight to experience in itself, but a distraction from silence.

Further along on our tour, a leopard seal swam around a sculptured iceberg as she dove for krill living on the underside. She must have been a younger seal because they eat mostly krill. The adults can be ten feet long or more, and they eat the smaller seals and their young. We rounded the seal's berg a couple of times and she swam over to check us out, perhaps for dinner possibilities. Fortunately, we flunked the test.

During one of the staff's lectures, we saw a filmed sequence in which a leopard seal grabbed a young penguin, and then thrashed it around in the water to remove the skin. I had to turn away from that awful violence. After recovering, I did recognize how efficiently the leopard seal removed the skin for its dinner. The wilderness is not always pretty, but it can be efficient.

Harriet dressed for extreme weather in the Neumeyer Channel, almost the furthest point south.

Nesting gentoo penguins amidst streaks of their ejected excrement.

CHAPTER 8

Pink Poop
and Adélie Thieves

Our naturalists educated us about penguins and their lives throughout our tour. After seeing the penguins' behavior firsthand and learning about their lives and habitats, I finally began to understand and appreciate the complexities of their lives and how they intertwine with the other wildlife. For one, they all depend on Antarctic krill, a necessary little creature in the sea's food supply. When a seal or penguin gorges on the pink krill, the liquid excrement is pink. Whales feasting on krill can end up with red poop. At night, swarms of krill feed on the phytoplankton that live on the underside of icebergs. During the day, most of the krill swim down into the ocean to three hundred feet to avoid predators, though enough remain on the bottom of the ice for krill-feeders to find a good meal. The larger the ice sheet, the greater the population of krill will be. In spite of the abundance of wildlife at the edge of Antarctica, the lack of variety makes them all incredibly fragile.

Bandit Adélies

Before my trip to Antarctica, I mentioned to a friend that I wanted to bring back rocks. She replied, "Oh, you can't do that. There are so few rocks that the penguins steal them from each other."

Once I observed penguin behavior on Paulet Island I learned that wasn't quite the case. The tightly packed Adélie penguin nests left only enough room between each personal bowl of rocks so that neighboring penguins could not conveniently steal the stones that kept the eggs and chicks off the wet ground. We walked around several old and unused nests constructed with the same size of stones as in the active nests, but the nesting penguins did not take any of those stones. They preferred to steal stones from nests in use and seemed to take delight when the nest's occupant objected to the pilfering. Maybe this gave the stolen stone higher value as a gift to the sitting parent.

It seemed to be more like a proof of pairing, dare I say love, than something required for construction. One of our guides said that a female Adélie might seduce a neighboring male into having intercourse with her, and while he is distracted she steals one of his rocks. Scientists have a number of theories for this behavior, but so far there is no consensus.

Penguins living in tight quarters have to put up with getting hit by explosive excrement from a neighbor, which can shoot up to ten feet from the source. Nests are two-to-six-feet apart, which means many penguins must sit for hours with white or pink streaks across their backs until their mate returns. Then they can go to the sea to bathe and eat. Early in the season when we visited, the pink dashes radiated out from each nest, making a Jackson Pollack-like design. People on their second or third tour of Antarctica told us that the patterns on the open space between the nests disappear as the guano builds to a pungent, knee-deep stew that stinks. Fortunately, we missed that stage. Some friends who had visited Antarctica later in the penguins' nesting season said they could not get rid of the revolting odor from their rubber boots, so they left their boots on the ship when they disembarked. No wonder the ship had so many boots to lend the new arrivals.

Neko Harbor on the Antarctic Continent

Loose, brash, ice-filled Neko Harbor was our second and last visit to the continent of Antarctica. Julio marveled that over the years few tourists have even stepped foot on the shore of Neko Harbor, perhaps only "enough to fill a couple of football stadiums." Most tourists have only visited the islands, as we had been doing, and the ones who come on the larger ships never even get to set foot on Antarctica.

Even though the shoreline looked like others we had seen, my feet tingled as I planted them on the thin, rocky strip of exposed rocks, very aware that I was standing on the edge of the Antarctic continent. I felt connected to Shackleton and the other explorers who could not have imagined that people like me would one day make a comfortable tour to places explorers once considered their most challenging destinations.

My friend Sally and I carefully picked our way along the steep slope covered in dirty old snow, hard from months on the ground and the passage of hundreds of gentoo penguins. They marched to the sea for food and then back to the nesting spots they used the previous year, even though we could only see the snow that covered them. Experienced penguin parents use sites on higher ground where flooding is less likely as the snow melts. An egg laid on snow will freeze, so the older penguin couples know to wait until the snow melts before preparing their nests for eggs. When their nest of pebbles emerges from the snow, they spend days moving the pebbles around until every placement suits them. Then they go on with their breeding activities.

Younger pairs or newly paired older adults that have lost their mates are left with less desirable sites for their nests. They may need time to construct a new nest from unused stones. Their chicks are hatched later and have a higher mortality rate due to the possibility of the chick drowning in the low-lying nest.

Sally and I passed a small red hut peeking out from a snow bank, built and maintained by the Argentines for emergencies. A pair of Snowy Sheathbills with their wings folded stood on the roof and watched us walk by, curious, and seemingly unafraid. The snowy sheathbill is the only land bird native to Antarctica. These omnivorous birds eat everything possible, including broken eggs, bird feces, afterbirth, and weak babies. They are small enough not to threaten the penguins and they keep the penguin colony clean. Snowy sheathbills breed at the same time as the penguins in order to feed their chicks nutrient-rich regurgitated krill brought to the colonies by busy penguins. Visually, the snowy sheathbills are one of the few birds I would describe as ugly. Their naked warty faces and sheaths cover half of their top bills. The two we saw had faces that looked like a partially picked scab.

Julio had warned us about softening patches of snow and, sure enough, as we walked up the slope Sally disappeared. One moment she was beside me and then she was gone. Well, not really. When she burst out laughing I looked down and saw her sprawled on the snow, one leg fully embraced by the icy crust. We managed to free her leg but had to sacrifice her rubber boot for a moment. I dug it out while she balanced on her booted foot. The hole did seem just the right size to trap a small penguin as Julio had warned. For example, an Adélie is 16 inches tall and 2.2 pounds, and it would just fill that hole, sentencing the unlucky bird to certain starvation. As Julio instructed, we filled in the hole by stomping on the surrounding crust and snow.

We continued our peaceful walk inland until the startling sound of a sharp crack made us jump. We turned to see our ship, tiny across the bay, paused at the base of the immense face of Rudolf Glacier. With another crack, a gigantic piece of ice slipped off the side of the glacier and plunged into Neko Harbor. The ice chunk popped out of the water and then bobbed up and down several times. The wave it spawned jerked the ship side to side, which must have been a thrill for the people on board! The wave rolled across the bay into the cove near us.

It took a moment for me to catch my breath after that spectacle. The peace and quiet soon returned and the bathing penguins did not miss a beat. For them, it's just life on the beach.

This was another astonishing event on this incredible continent!

Gentoos Bathing, Playing & Hunting

After our stroll inland, Sally and I returned to the shoreline where masses of gentoo penguins were bathing, much like robins do in a puddle. The penguins tossed upward sprays of water and fluttered their flippers. I picked my bird to watch. She floated on the surface and swished her tail with vigor to clean her nether regions. She lay on one side to swish and splash, her upward flipper high in the air, and then she turned to the other side for another good swish until she felt properly cleaned. She picked at stubborn stains on her belly and finished with a good preening, getting every feather in its proper alignment to capture the right amount of air needed for good buoyancy.

When my penguin finished her bathing, she slid underwater to swim as fast as a bird can fly. The extraordinarily clear water in the bay made it easy to watch her streaking among the others, and then zip away further out into the bay. She joined hundreds of penguins all surfacing with a brief jump out of the sea to snatch some air, and then diving back down under the water. They stroked their flippers in both directions to give them momentum, like sculling. The gentoos almost looked as if they were normal birds flying through the air, exuding joy with each playful leap. There seemed to be no practical purpose to the antics other than just having fun.

On further reflection, I realized that besides jumping out of the water for air, hunger drove the gentoos on their way to speedily reach their feeding grounds. I try not to anthropomorphize wildlife, but sometimes it's impossible not to project my own excitement onto their exuberance that I interpret as playful fun.

Back on the ship, the crew served us barbeque on the back deck. The protected harbor's weather was relatively pleasant, and although the sun was not really warm, it seemed like a real picnic. After the meal, I moved to the foredeck to watch the landscape as we sailed out of Neko Harbor.

A patch of churning water appeared ahead of our ship and as we drew closer we saw leaping penguins, which caused the disturbance. These penguins looked like the ones I had seen from the shore on their way to their feeding grounds at full speed. Penguins travel in large numbers as a safety measure to foil predators, similar to what migrating birds do. When moving fast in the open sea, hundreds of little bodies leaping out of the water create churning surface waters. From a distance, the water appears to be boiling. It must also be confusing to a lurking leopard seal, which is the point, of course.

A Glimpse of the Most Scenic Place on Earth

The same day we visited Neko Harbor our schedule included a cruise through Lemaire Channel, claimed by some to be the most scenic place on earth. At the south end of the South Shetland Islands, a number of large and small islands form many channels. We passed through Neumayer Channel, a canyon of high cliffs partially obscured by fog. The ship's bow pushed aside floating ice chunks until we broke out into a short section of ice-free water exposed to our right. A short distance ahead of us was Lemaire Channel.

I wanted the closest view possible of this channel because it would be our furthest point south. I suited up with every bit of warm clothing I had, including my fleece-lined cap with earflaps, in order to face the bitter winds. A few other hardy people were already on the bow prepared to see the incredible beauty. Low clouds hung in this channel as well, but below the clouds, bright beams of sunlight beckoned to us from the far end, a mystical emanation of its own. The ship slowed as our patch of clear water ran out. Moving chunks of brash ice pressed tightly together, barring our passage. Whipped by the chilly wind, yet mesmerized by the sun that seemed just within reach, the handful of us on deck gloried at the sight, imperfect though it was.

Wind blows the big icebergs, the smaller "bergy bits," and the slushy brash ice around the Antarctic continent. If the wind pushes the large pieces of floating ice together, the mass can freeze solid. This is called pack ice and it can form when the surface temperature of the water is near freezing, which it usually is in Antarctica. Another type of ice called "fast ice" is similar, but it either grows from the shoreline or connects to the shore after forming on the surface of the seawater. In either case, if this happens when a ship is surrounded by the pack, the ship is immobilized. Ship captains are aware of the possibility of being trapped by the shifting ice, which is what happened to *Clipper Adventurer* two years before our trip. Fortunately, an icebreaker happened to be in the area and rescued the ship.

The loudspeaker startled me out of my trance. "This is Julio. I am so sorry to announce that we will not be moving any further south. We cannot risk the possibility of being frozen in this pack ice, so we will be heading back to shelter for the night."

The captain of *Clipper Adventurer* put the ship in reverse and slowly turned around, leaving "the most scenic place on earth" behind us. He was not going to take any chances this time.

We on the bow agreed that it was a good decision. My disappointment at not experiencing the full impact of this legendary channel dissipated with relief as I considered the captain's decision. My agenda for the trip did not include becoming ice-locked, even for a few days. Once again, I was reminded that especially in wild and remote places, itineraries are only possibilities.

The warmth of the ship's salon and a cup of cocoa called to me. I glanced back once more at the forbidden channel, awe struck by the raw magnificence and my great fortune to witness it. I reminded myself, *I am standing deep in the Antarctic, a place so unfriendly that most of this enormous continent has not been explored, seen, or exploited—and much of it never will.*

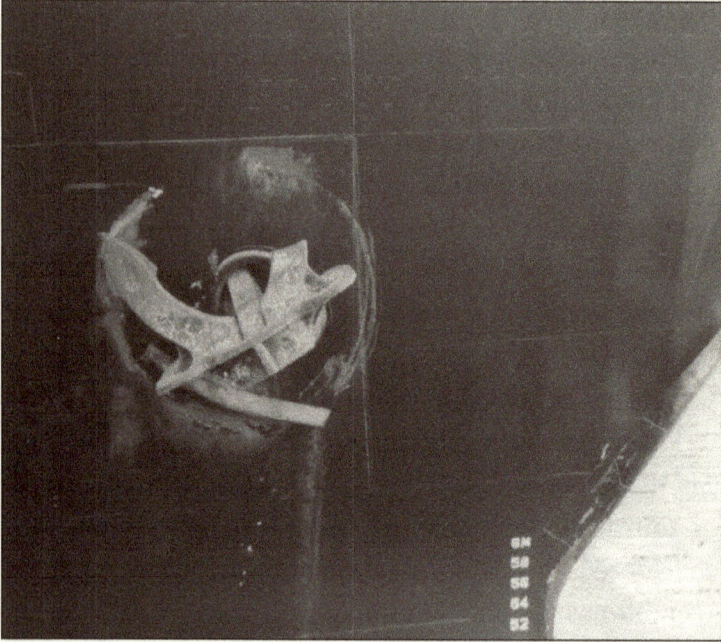

The ship's anchor, broken in the storm that hit on the last night.

CHAPTER 9

A Stormy Finale

After the relatively easy voyage south across Drake Passage to Antarctica, all of us hoped for similar good luck crossing that passage to Ushuaia, Argentina where our trip ended. But the return north was another story. At the end of our last day of exploring the Antarctic Peninsula, the captain of *Clipper Adventurer* cancelled our scheduled landing at Port Lockroy on Goudier Island due to high wind and fog.

The next morning we awoke to howling wind and learned that the previous night it had gusted to 80 knots, hurricane force winds. While we slept, the anchor fluke, which had been dug into the sea bottom to hold the ship, broke off. The ship's motion had calmed briefly as the ship floated untethered toward another shore, pushed by the raging wind. The crew had to turn out of their warm bunks in the middle of the night to get us safely under way. The passengers knew nothing of that midnight work party until we found a digital photo on the bulletin board the next morning that showed the wounded anchor hanging off the bow.

The photos reminded me of the few times in Mexico on our sailboat when our anchor failed us. While at anchor, the boat fought against the powerful wind, seeking release, jerking back and forth like a dog at the end of a leash. And when the anchor pulled free, the motion quieted with the boat no longer held to the ocean floor. Familiar with what that meant, we would jump into motion to set sail and gain control of the situation. What an adrenaline high that was—one I'd rather not experience too often!

After gearing up in my warm clothes, I pushed my way onto the wind blown deck and leaned over the bow rail to take a photo of that sad looking, rusty piece of metal that had been our anchor. I've seen a retired anchor like that outside of a restaurant on the Oregon coast. The shank was at least five feet long, two flukes going one way, and a bar at a ninety-degree angle. I wondered how old our anchor might have been since most anchors I've seen on large ships are a different shape.

After breakfast, I climbed up into the wheel-house, called the "bridge" on big ships and found the captain consulting with a few experienced crew-members. The captain welcomed passengers to sit in a two-seat bench right behind the helm, so I crept in and watched. Julio studied the latest weather map with the captain. Their pinched faces spoke volumes. I heard our experienced expedition director, Julio, admit, "Captain, you are worrying me."

Earlier, I had noticed that the weather map next to the dining room showed a serious, low weather front bearing down on our course to Tierra del Fuego. In the wheelhouse, the barometer needle dropped off the scale past "L," indicating that the weather had begun to change already. *Not good,* I thought. A low-pressure front will suck air from the surrounding areas of higher pressure and if the pressure difference is extreme, as ours was, the resulting winds could be very strong, even to hurricane strength.

The captain sheltered the ship behind the South Shetland Islands while Julio kept the passengers informed through the intercom. We learned that the scheduled Zodiac tour had been cancelled, which was fine with me, given the circumstances. High winds on a rubber boat meant a bumpy ride and lots of splashing, at the very least.

We gathered in small groups offering one another reassurance. I drew courage from seasoned passengers who said we would be fine. The captain had decided to begin the journey to South America earlier than planned in case we needed extra time to safely cross the notoriously angry waters of Drake Passage. So, I put my faith in the captain and resolved to enjoy the adventure. I'd sailed in rough water in a much smaller boat, so I reassured myself. *How bad could it get?* Little did I know.

Plunging into the Wild Ocean

Our destination was Tierra del Fuego, which lay about 500 miles to the north. Around eleven in the morning the captain navigated the ship out of our protective bay and pointed the bow north. Out the stern windows I watched the shadow of land fade into thick fog. I snatched another scopolamine patch and stuck it behind my ear to ward off nausea. At lunch, I lightly commented that it might be the last food I could eat for a while—it was.

While we ate, the crew prepared the ship. They tightened the lashings holding everything on deck, from the chairs to the Zodiacs. A crewmember closed and bolted the single porthole cover in my cabin. The porthole's heavy, steel cover blocked my view of the ocean, and considering the predicted weather, I counted myself as lucky. The porthole could be under water in the stormy seas, which would not be an encouraging view while I languished in my bunk with motion sickness. The crew told us to secure loose items in our cabins, preferably on the floor, so they wouldn't be thrown about and broken. I shoved the clutter from my desk and nightstand into my duffle bag and pushed it under the bed.

Before long, the ship's motion became more extreme and I began a two-day marathon of naps. In my cozy dark hole, night and day became irrelevant. Any time I woke up, I knew whether it was just a nap or a night's sleep because when I napped, I only threw the spare blanket over me. At night, I got into the bed and under the covers. I felt that some protocol must be maintained, even in the worst of conditions.

Shipboard activities continued although fewer and fewer people showed up for the lectures in the main lounge. I knew the lounge was the worst place to be when the ship pitched forward and back, and rolled side to side. Fortunately, Julio arranged for the lectures to be broadcast over the cabin speakers. Despite the turbulent seas, the lectures were still interesting. Several scientists on the ship's lecture team had spent summers or long winters in the Antarctic region doing research, most of them far inland. Their insights gave us a good sense of the interior of the barren continent, its resources, and the challenges for humans to live there, even with modern equipment and conveniences.

I snuggled into my warm nest, listened for a while, and then took another nap.

Occasionally, I ventured out to test the state of my stomach by joining people in the lounge. The number of robust passengers dwindled each time I emerged. Sometimes, snacks appeared, easy on the stomach and quick to eat in case the ship jerked. I'd get another ginger ale and before long, a horizontal position in private seemed best.

During my waking moments in bed, I interpreted the ship's motion, recalling a previous experience weathering 40-knot winds on the open sea off Cabo San Lucas, Mexico, in our 25-foot sailboat *Valhalla*. On *Clipper Adventurer,* the head of my bed abutted the hull, so I rolled side to side as the ship pitched forward and back. I could visualize the waves almost taller than the ship, pushing our craft away as it climbed up the wall of water and I rolled to the right. When the wave passed under the hull, the ship slid down into the trough and I rolled to the left. If the ship rolled side to side at all, I slid toward my pillow, and then down toward my feet in my bed. The intensity of the motion came in cycles, starting soft then building to a real doozy, then softening again as waves on a summer sea will do.

Another Rough Day at Sea

Early on the second day of wild wind and seas, I felt a change in the ship's motion and actually stayed up for a while. From experience, I knew the best thing for seasickness is to look at the horizon, so I dragged myself up four flights of stairs to the wheelhouse where our stalwart captain, surrounded by instruments and a few crew, stood in command of the ship. Enormous waves rolled into the port quarter, lifting the ship until its bow pointed above the horizon. When the ship reached the tipping point on the crest it pitched forward and slid down the face of the wave as if to continue right down to the bottom of the sea. At the last second, the bow lifted to climb the next wave, sending spray high up over the bow. The roller coaster thrilled me as long as I kept the faith that the ship would actually recover and not just keep descending into the depths.

One of the heartier observers that day told me that the previous afternoon a giant wave had broken over the wheelhouse windows forty feet or so above the roiling surface of the sea. Sobering. The winds had gusted to Force 12 on the Beaufort Wind Scale, a wind measurement mariners developed for recording wind speeds in the open ocean. Force 12 is the highest wind velocity on the scale and considered hurricane force.

That day on *Clipper Adventurer* we were certainly in the open ocean. Steady winds at force 9, 45 knots, (52 mph), and frequent higher gusts battered the ship. These winds had whipped the sea into chaos all the way from the South American continent—not a great consolation for me at the time. I had the same mix of terror, excitement, and serene fatalism as I watched the drama through the wheelhouse window.

The turmoil brought to mind my last experience with force 10 winds (60 mph). My husband at the time and I had anchored our 25-foot sailboat in Mazatlan Harbor, prepared for hurricane weather. We battened down the hatches and watched and waited. As the wind increased, we watched an unoccupied sailboat about the same size as our boat, break loose from its anchor and batter itself against an overhang and sink. Our dingy sank, still tied to the boat, unable to break free from the thrashing stern. Our main anchor line broke. We thought it was the end, but it wasn't. The #2 anchor, put out just in case, grabbed us and held us in the middle of the harbor. In our sailboat's little cabin, I used my *Chapman's Piloting and Seamanship* to determine the wind's velocity by using the book's photos of waves created by the various velocities and looking out the cabin window at what we faced.

So, riding out this storm in a larger ship with a competent, experienced crew felt almost safe in comparison to my experience in Mazatlan Harbor. Off-duty crewmembers trickled in to the wheelhouse to watch the action. Most had never been in seas that rough, and the ones who had, shared their tales in soft voices, making it hard for me to hear cautionary tales. Looking out that window at the feared waters of Drake Passage, I was happy to let the captain worry about speeds, angles, and ETAs for our landfall. I was relieved to know I could go below to my cabin, trust the captain's navigational skills, and nap. It would soon be over.

Late that night, I felt the ship's motion calm a little and when the tinny voice on the intercom announced Bananas Foster had been served in the lounge, I threw back the covers. Num! The warm banana was mighty tasty smothered in sweet sauce and topped with a bit of liqueur, along with a spoonful of ice cream. And better yet, it stayed down.

Calm Seas

On the morning of the third and last day of the stormy passage, the winds had moderated enough for the dining room to open again. For my first meal after my ginger-ale diet, the staff valiantly served what food could safely be prepared. We sat at tables grabbing objects as they slid across the white tablecloth. Before long, the waiter dampened the tablecloths and this helped deter slippage. Then the ship lurched and the waiter jammed his thigh against our table to steady himself. A loud crash from across the dining room disrupted the relative calm. I thought a window had blown out. A side table full of juice pitchers and bowls spilled onto the floor, scattering glass and liquid everywhere. A moment later, the ship took another deep roll at the same time one of the crew opened the door to a refrigerator only ten feet from us. He fell to the ground and all the contents flew into his lap. Indeed, some crewmembers learned important lessons in this storm.

The winds subsided throughout the day and finally, we gained the shelter of Cape Horn, the southernmost point of South America. Soon, we tied up to the dock, safe in Ushuaia Harbor, the capital of Tierra del Fuego, Argentina, and the southern most city in the world. Our dramatic crossing completed a fabulous trip.

CHAPTER 10

Changing Times

More than fifteen years after this adventure, I mostly remember Antarctica's isolation and its pristine landscape, rarely marred with a human structure. The humbling sight from shore of an enormous glacier dwarfing our ship as it anchored in one of the bays is also unforgettable. Crystal clear water, hanging ice cliffs, and floating icebergs all took my breath away with their beauty while also pulsing with potential danger. For me, there were many reminders of early explorers who endured the wild storms, bitter cold, treacherous ice, menacing meat-eating seals, and starvation. Some explorers died and others survived. I am fortunate to have witnessed the Antarctic firsthand, see these places explorers described in their accounts, and return safely in relative comfort.

Amidst the spellbinding scenery, the wildlife that thrives on the edge of that forbidding continent is unforgettable. It is humbling to understand the incredible adaptations that Antarctic polar species have undergone to live in such an unforgiving land. Just watching a sleepy crabeater seal raise his curious head off his iceberg and my knowing that he never goes ashore, boggled my mind. As humans, we are such land-oriented creatures, and there I was, observing an animal that never even thinks of land as part of his world.

While I feel fortunate to have traveled to Antarctica, the continent now faces challenges to control the tourism boom. In 2009, the Falklands received 69,000 visitors, many on enormous cruise ships that carried up to 5,000 passengers. That same year, the International Association of Antarctic Tourism Operators (IAATO) prohibited the large ships from visiting most of the Antarctic Peninsula for fear of an accident and resulting oil spills. None of these cruise ships had a reinforced hull like our small ship. Now, most ships allowed to travel to Antarctica carry fewer than 200 passengers.

The Falklands have also made progress to protect its archipelago. After signing the U.N. Landmine Treaty in 2010, the British returned with greater resolve to remove the landmines planted during the war in the Falklands. The once small landmine museum in Stanley has been expanded to cover more of the history of the Falklands and give visitors a broader understanding of this part of the world.

In 2014, cruise ships brought about 40,000 passengers to the Falklands and the ships now pay a per-passenger fee for docking for the night. These fees have enriched the Falklands' overall revenue, in turn more than making up for the decline in revenue from wool sales, fishing, and other small industries. Given the increased market for clothing made with natural fibers, I wonder if the wool market might even recover. In addition, farmers on the islands can now depend on monthly deliveries by inter-island shipping services, and light seaplanes service the islands for emergencies.

South Pole Ambassador

Frank Todd, Ph.D., is an Antarctic historian and photographer who has given a title to those of us fortunate enough to have visited the Antarctic, and now, passionately advocate for its protection. We have become "South Polar Ambassadors." Now, we sing the Antarctic's praises and advocate for its protection. As Todd so aptly said:

"That such a wondrous and unspoiled place still exists on this beleaguered planet is one of the real miracles of the 20th century. The indescribable splendor of the magnificent final frontier and its remarkable wildlife must be forever regarded as an irreplaceable international treasure that justly deserves to be protected indefinitely for future generations."

As an ambassador, I know I need to make more people aware of the Antarctic and the continent of Antarctica and the environmental threats to this part of the world and its wildlife. Admittedly, I am terrified to know that almost all of the Antarctic wildlife depends on billions of tiny krill, the foundation of the food chain. Krill is so fragile, yet so essential, and if the ice melts in the future, wildlife dependent on krill must be able to adapt or they will die off—

just as other species in crises have done in the past. With today's discouraging climate change predictions, I wonder, *What can replace krill in time to feed all the wildlife so dependent on this food source?*

On the other end of the climate change spectrum, I am deeply concerned about scientists' 2013 discovery that there is a major rift at the base of the ice shelf 20 miles inland on the Pine Island Glacier in West Antarctica. In 2015, a 224-square-mile iceberg broke off from the glacier. Warming ocean temperatures have caused the glacier to crack from the inside out—a surprise to scientists. If this trend continues, the ice sheet could collapse within decades, causing a predicted 10-foot rise in global sea levels and massive coastal flooding that puts cities like Miami and New York City underwater. "It's no longer a question of whether the ...ice sheet *will* melt, it's a question of when," declared Ian Howat, Ph.D., a glaciologist and earth sciences professor at Ohio State University.

From the krill to the glaciers, the Antarctic region and the continent of Antarctica must be protected against the onslaught of humanity and our negative environmental impact.

I was fortunate to have the opportunity to indulge my curiosity and feed my passion for Antarctica, such a fascinating and dangerously bedazzling place. At the same time, I am heartbroken that it could all be lost. As a South Polar Ambassador, I will do what I can to prevent that by supporting the work to prevent further climate change, which is the underlying cause for the disintegration of the ice on Antarctica. Sharing my experiences in Antarctica and speaking out for its protection are the least I can do as a South Polar Ambassador.

Madagascar
AFRICA

2004

Routes crossing
MADAGASCAR

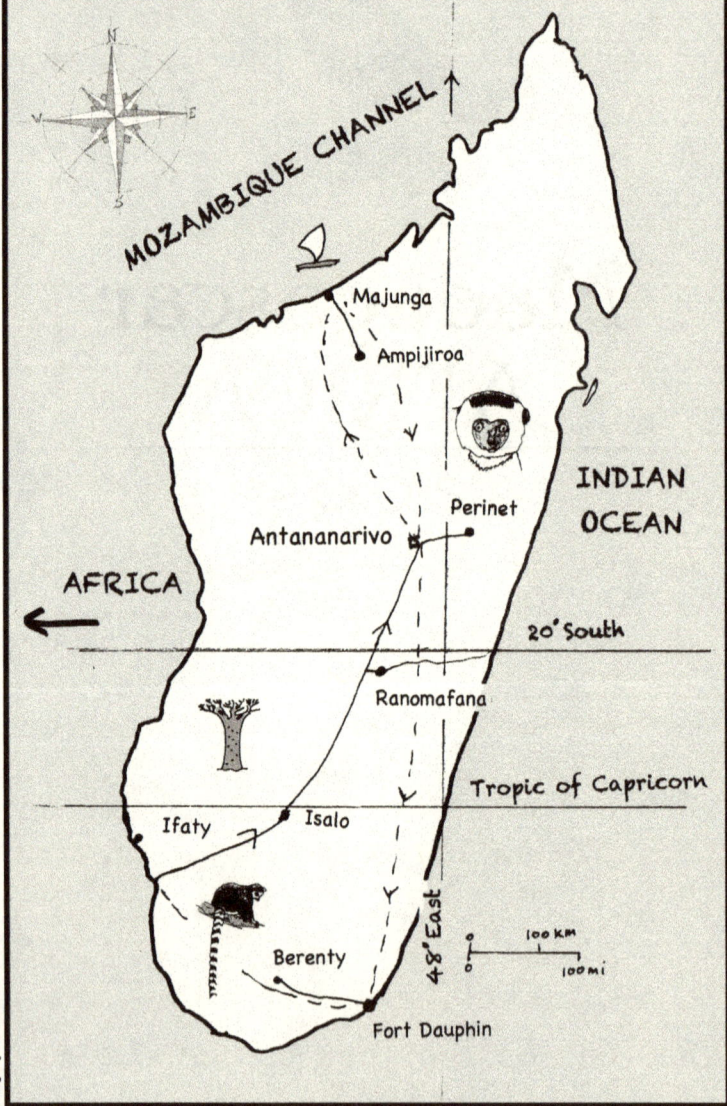

MOZAMBIQUE CHANNEL

Majunga

Ampijiroa

INDIAN
OCEAN

Perinet

Antananarivo

AFRICA

20° South

Ranomafana

Tropic of Capricorn

Ifaty   Isalo

48° East

Berenty

100 KM

100 mi

Fort Dauphin

Map by Harriet Denison

Introduction

A few months after my 2001 tour to Antarctica, I shared lunch with four new friends from that trip. After thoroughly discussing our previous excursion, reminiscing about the exciting times and difficult moments, someone boldly asked, "Where to next?"

Immediately, I said, "Madagascar!" And another friend chimed in, "Yes, Madagascar!"

It was the lemurs that drew me to Madagascar. Sweet, cute, and silly in all the photos and videos I had seen. The opportunity to be in their presence and to watch them just be themselves in their natural habitat seemed like an incredible adventure. Our enthusiasm infected the other women at lunch and the unanimous decision to visit that remote and mysterious land made us giddy with excitement.

Then I did some research. Alison Jolly Ph.D., a zoologist and a primatologist known for her studies of lemur biology, had studied lemurs in Madagascar for 25 years and was the first one to propose female dominance in a primate society. I liked that connection. She wrote the following in a fascinating, but discouraging article in the February 1987 issue of *National Geographic:*

> Madagascar has more than enough fertile land left to feed its people if the land is farmed for high yield. **And with proper management,** enough forest still stands to make Madagascar self-sufficient in fuel as well as to preserve most of its unique plants and animals. [Author's bold for emphasis.]

Sadly, later reports confirmed that Dr. Jolly's suggestions had been ignored. As I considered actually going to Madagascar, I knew this country's fragile environment had already been overrun by a growing population. My tumultuous inner arguments went on and on. *Go now before there is nothing left to see,* and then, *Go now to validate that saving what wildlife remains could bring money to a desperately poor country.*

But then, my inner debate turned to this: Tourism can be a mixed blessing, as other developing countries have discovered; tourists can "love" a fascinating and beautiful place to ruin.

Ultimately, I decided I had to go. *The opportunity will never come again,* I told myself.

A friend had recommended Mark Smith, a Portland-based leader of nature tours, who offered a three-week tour of Madagascar that promised both lemurs and birds as well as other unusual creatures that would certainly cross our paths. This seemed like the best optio for my fellow travelers and me.

It took three years for all of our schedules to finally mesh, but early in 2004 we signed up for the October nature tour. In the end, this became a trip that stands out as one of the most extraordinary journeys in my many years of worldwide travel.

What Makes Madagascar So Unusual?

Madagascar is the fourth largest island in the world, and is about twice the size of Arizona. In grade school, I remember noticing that the opposing shorelines of Madagascar and the east coast of Africa fit together like pieces of a puzzle. What a surprise to learn that it was once a part of Gondwanaland, the ancient landmass that broke apart some 180 million years ago and became Africa, Antarctica, South America, Australia, and the Indian subcontinent. My childhood observation was correct.

Madagascar is now located in the Indian Ocean, directly east of the African country of Mozambique. The wildlife that existed on that drifting scrap of land evolved, isolated from relatives on the larger continents of Africa and Asia. According to current scientific thought, additional animals and plants that now live in Madagascar may have floated across from Africa on storm-ripped trees, adding diversity to the slowly changing populations of flora and fauna on Madagascar.

Lemurs are only found on Madagascar and scientists believe they are descendants of the pre-primates of Gondwanaland. At least half of all species of lemurs once in existence are recorded only from fossils. Scientists speculate that one ancient lemur weighed up to 440 pounds. Today, 101 species and subspecies of lemurs survive on Madagascar and all are endangered.

Of the 258 bird species identified on Madagascar, 115 are endemic, meaning they are found only on this island. In addition, 90 percent of the island's known living species are endemic, making Madagascar one of the most ecologically diverse places on earth.

Early Inhabitants

Before the first settlers arrived, a variety of habitats covered Madagascar, from desert scrub in the south to tropical dry forest further north and west, and tropical rainforest near the eastern coast. Today, 80 percent of Madagascar is barren due to repeated plowing and intentional fires that support subsistence farming.

Scientists are still researching the early human history of Madagascar. Anthropologists believe the first migrants arrived from Borneo, Indonesia about two thousand years ago, sailing in outrigger canoes on the same trade winds used by their merchant-ancestors. Over many years, the earliest settlers found the island's central highlands to be the best land for growing the rice they brought with them from Borneo, so this is where they eventually concentrated their tribal settlements. In the mid 1500s, the most powerful chief, Andriamanelo, united the highland tribes into one group called the Merinas, which is now the most politically powerful ethnic group in Madagascar.

Remnants of 9th century coastal fortifications built by Arab traders are the oldest signs of occupancy, and Europeans later built forts there to protect their own interests in the trade among Africa, the Middle East, and Asia.

The name Madagascar emerged when Marco Polo landed there in the 13th century. He thought he had landed near Mogadishu in Somalia on the east African coast, an active port for Arab traders at the time. The name "Madagascar" is a corruption of "Mogadishu," but the name stuck, and it gained popularity during the Middle Ages.

The Bantus from East Africa sailed to Madagascar about one thousand years ago and first settled on the northwest coast then migrated to other coasts. In the early 17th century, the Merinas subdued the scattered Bantu tribes and ruled the island until the 1800s. As conquerors, the Merinas forced the Bantus to work as slaves and sold them into the slave trade.

The first Europeans attempted settlements on Madagascar in the 1600s, but with limited success. European Christian missionaries came and went, depending on the favor of the ruling Merina monarch. In the early 1800s, the Merinas controlled all of Madagascar, and had repelled and discouraged incursions by the French and the British who both wanted a permanent port on Madagascar in order to support their trading ships bound for India. During that period of global European colonization, the French and British negotiated the control of two islands they both claimed, Madagascar and Zanzibar. They agreed that Madagascar would be under French control in return for the French ceding to the British control of Zanzibar, an important trading island off the coast of East Africa.

These negotiations had occurred without including the Merinas who were furious at the arrangement, but helpless to change it even though they tried. The Merinas cancelled trading concessions with France, which precipitated the Franco-Hova Wars that resulted in two French invasions into the heart of Merina territory in 1883 and 1890. The Merina rule crumbled and Queen Ranavalona III signed an agreement accepting the foreign influence in Madagascar. It became a French protectorate in 1895, opening the island to colonialization. In 1948 as colonialism waned, the French began a peaceful transition toward independence for Madagascar, culminating in full independence in 1960.

Today, there are about eighteen ethnicities represented in Madagascar's population, and the largest group is the powerful Merinas, comprising 25 percent of the population. The official languages are now French and Malagasy, and many people also speak English. The year we visited, Madagascar had a population of 17 million people with 73 percent living in rural areas.

Diverse but Fragile Ecosystems

Researchers now flock to Madagascar hoping to discover another Rosy Periwinkle, a plant native to Madagascar that provided important ingredients for fighting certain forms of cancer. In spite of the intense research to date, the unique flora and fauna of Madagascar still hide their mysteries. However, as fast as scientists discover a new species another habitat is degraded. The more I learned about Madagascar, the more I felt driven to visit this unique place on the planet before it was too late. So in 2005, three years after that decisive lunch with friends in Portland, we began our journey to Madagascar.

Crested Drongo

Royal Hill, the historic spiritual hub for the Malagasy people, near Antananarivo

CHAPTER I

Northwest Madagascar

Travel to Madagascar was an arduous trip by modern standards, including two, ten-hour flights and a long layover in Paris, yet I was excited for almost three weeks of adventure. We were jet lagged when our tour group of fourteen birders arrived in Antananarivo, the capital of Madagascar and its largest city with 5.4 million people. We dragged ourselves off the plane, prepared to take one more short flight to our first destination and a much-needed nap. Immediately, we hit a snag. Our tour guide, Mark Smith, gathered us together in the almost deserted, open-air airport to explain the situation.

"OK, here's our first bump," Mark lamented. "Not surprisingly, we will not all be able to take the next plane to Majunga."

My spirits dropped, I so wanted to lie down and sleep.

"I tried to pick up our tickets for the next leg of our trip," Mark continued, "and the agent informed me that only half of us can go on the next plane, but there is another plane this afternoon."

There goes the lovely snooze by a peaceful beach, I thought. The other thirteen experienced travelers did not seem bothered at all, so I had a little chat with myself. *Things happen. You have to change gears.*

This was only my second international birding trip with an organized tour. On my first trip to Antarctica, we lived on the ship and went ashore for excursions, which was very different from being part of a group that moved around mostly by plane and bus. I realized we all needed to be considerate when the plans changed. I was not travelling alone.

Chipper, as a guide must be, Mark continued, "It's something about having too many people getting off in Majunga where we are going, and no one getting on the plane at that stop for the Comoros Islands, the plane's next stop. But don't worry, I've made arrangements so we will all be together by this evening."

Mark had led many tours to Madagascar, and later in our trip, his remarkable ability to find and identify birds, matched by his keen interest in other wildlife and plants, impressed me. That first day, I concluded that he could also cope with the irregularities we would face, so I relaxed, and waited to see what came next.

Holding a handful of plane tickets in the air, Mark said, "I have tickets for those of you who will fly out in two hours, and the others will spend the day here in Antananarivo. We will have time for a nap and maybe take a tour this afternoon. Then we will follow on the next flight to Majunga."

A small, dark man with a big grin joined our circle. "Oh, good to see you Rivo." Mark said. They shook hands with a half man-hug and backslapping. "Hey, everyone, this is Rivo Rarivosoa, our in-country guide. He knows the birds, the animals, and better yet, the local languages to deal with bumps in the road like this one. Nothing goes as planned in Madagascar, so be warned."

Mark smiled, relieved to have our local guide with us. Rivo nodded in agreement, acknowledging his comfort in dealing with irregularities like this.

In the following days, I learned that Rivo was an excellent naturalist and proficient in English, French, Malagasy, and Japanese. He also has a good sense of humor that proved to be an asset in dealing with our diverse group. Among us, we had a range of enthusiasm and personal agendas for the trip—from eager birders to avid photographers to parents who just liked to travel with their adult daughter. I was surprised to find myself among the more serious birders, especially since I certainly was not a seasoned birder.

In time, we learned that traveling throughout Madagascar is expensive, time consuming, frustrating, and exciting. During our tour, we would take four interior flights on Air Madagascar in order to see a variety of ecosystems in a reasonable time frame. The airline is safe, though frequent schedule changes disrupted our planned itinerary. The government had changed the name of Madagascar Air to Air Madagascar in 1962 because the locals had nicknamed their national airline "Mad Air," adding levity as well as chagrin to the inevitable disruptions.

Royal Hill, Seat of Culture

Rivo took half of our tour group and left on the scheduled flight. I stayed behind with Mark and the others for a short nap at a nearby motel. After some food—no one knew what meal it was—we had time for a tour of Ambohimanga, a World Heritage site close to Antananarivo. This traditional fortified royal settlement is the oldest spiritual site in Madagascar. For many years, this site was off limits to foreigners because it is regarded as a sacred area, but the regulations had recently changed to allow tours like ours the privilege of a visit. Now this site draws a constant flow of pilgrims and tourists throughout the year, though the day we visited the grounds seemed empty.

The sacred nature of the ancestors buried in the royal tombs made Royal Hill at Ambohimanga the hub of the well-developed Merina civilization and the center of their tribal identity and spirituality between the 15th and 19th centuries. It is recognized throughout the world as the seat of a notable dynasty from 1817 until the present. Today, the Merinas' spiritual beliefs still include a strong sense that the spirits of the ancestors reside in the tombs in order to watch over those still living.

My photos did not capture the feeling of impregnability of the tall massive walls of Royal Hill, which withstood numerous attacks until Merina rule prevailed. The stone and plastered walls loomed over us as we trudged up toward them in the intense heat. Once gleaming, the whitewashed walls showed the gray and black streaks of mold from tropical rains and constant moisture. Nicely laid out walkways lacked the lovely vegetation that I imagined filled the empty dirt spaces when the royalty resided here many years ago. The wooden buildings inside the compound badly needed attention. (Fortunately, since our visit in 2004, some of those buildings have been restored to their original condition.)

Outside the high walls, a pair of giggling children caught my attention. A boy and a girl played together, both about three years old with chubby cheeks and bright smiles. They sat in a recessed doorway across a narrow cobbled street from some simply constructed souvenir shops. Their mother, one of the vendors, had dressed the children in sturdy clean clothes and lovingly placed a fly deterrent of rawhide on each of their heads. When the kids moved, clean hair from a cow's tail woven into the edges of the a leather headband disturbed the flies attempting to home in on the moist eyes of the youngsters. Their mother's care saved them from eye infections spread by flies desperate for any liquid in that dry environment.

As we approached the stall, the mother said something to the children and then turned to us, trying to engage our interest. She pointed to the toys on her tray wrapped in plastic bags. They were unique and quite cleverly made. For example, one craftsperson had created a tiny delivery van by removing the top and bottom of a Coke can, flattening it, and folding it so that the "Coca Cola" label ran across the toy van's roof. I wanted to buy one but we had a three-week tour ahead of us, and the toys looked too fragile to survive the journey.

The Port of Majunga

In Majunga, we rejoined the others in our group who had enjoyed a relaxing afternoon. Our hotel was the first of several French-managed hotels where tourists expect late dinners. We were tired and hungry in spite of the early hour and I felt a bit grumpy, too. The kitchen was not yet open, so Mark urged the French-trained staff to prepare something for us to eat—to my great relief.

Majunga, located on the northwest coast of Madagascar, is also known as Mahajanga. A number of high-end destination resorts have been built there for vacationing scuba divers primarily from France and the Scandinavian countries. We stayed in Majunga because the park we planned to visit the next day, three hours to the south, did not have accommodations for tourists.

Majunga served as a port for early trade ships sailing between Europe and India, and as a result, it has one of the most diverse populations in Madagascar, including descendants of Arabian, Portuguese, French, and Indian sailors. Unfortunately, the city lies in the direct path of annual hurricanes. Several years before our visit, monster storms hit the region and many people evacuated inland. Some returned slowly once rebuilding was allowed. (As of 2013, about 220,000 people live in Majunga.)

Over dinner, there was lots of lively conversation as we caught up with the day's activities. At one point, Mark stood to get our attention. He cleared his throat and announced in an energetic voice, "This is a good time to tell you what we have planned for tomorrow. We will be visiting Ankarafantsike National Park, which is located in a tropical dry forest."

We learned that these forests exist where there is lots of rain but a long dry season. The deciduous trees and shrubs survive the dry season by shedding their leaves, similar to our oaks and maples in the United States. In the tropical dry forests, the wildlife is as unique as the environs. Mark emphasized that we were in for some spectacular birding, assuring us, "Some of the birds we will see are only found in this type of ecosystem."

Oh, boy, I thought, *so unusual. My favorite kind of place!*

After a few questions, Mark then told us, "So, we'll have to get up at 3 a.m. in order to be at the park at dawn."

Of course! I thought. *The local birding I did at home prepared me for this. Birds get up at dawn and we have to be there for their first songs. But 3 a.m.? We just got here and I'm still exhausted.*

In one voice and without hesitation, the entire group groaned, "No."

Mark seemed taken aback at our collective response.

While we ate, he disappeared and returned just as we polished off our sweet gelatin dessert.

"Alright, the wonky airline schedule can accommodate our change of plans for our next flight out of here." Then he happily added, "So, we can go to the dry forest the day after tomorrow, and still be able to do everything we had planned to do."

We all sighed with relief, then staggered off to our beds.

Our First Birds in Madagascar

The first morning in Majunga I awoke to a delightful birdsong that wafted through my open window. After breakfast while we birded on the grounds, once again

I heard the lovely song that had awakened me. Mark pointed out a dark bird the size of a robin that had a glossy black head and erect forehead feathers. Mark called it the ubiquitous Crested Drongo, a common bird that we saw throughout Madagascar. The drongo is not a spectacular bird to see, but his melodious dawn song is glorious, which is often the case in the bird world. It seems birds either have brilliant feathers or a glorious song—but usually not both.

Our hotel in Majunga was located right on the beach with lovely swaying palms that provided shade for our relaxation and recovery after the grueling trip to reach Madagascar. Small fishing boats glided past our hotel at dawn on their way to the reefs. One boat sailed quite close to shore and I could clearly see the fisherman sitting comfortably in the stern, steering with one bare foot on the tiller. The triangular sail hung diagonally from a single boom fastened high on a loosely stepped mast. Outriggers added stability to the narrow, twenty-foot hull. The whole rig is called a lateen rig. These boats are a smaller version of the ancient trading *dhows* that Arabian traders used on their trips between Asia and Africa. Eventually, this style of boat brought the first humans to live on Madagascar.

We toured the lively seaport of Majunga, noting the busy fishing fleet just back from a morning at sea and the freighters anchored out in the deep waters of the bay waiting to offload their cargoes. At the thriving market, people wandered, chatted, and inspected items for sale. Men wore t-shirts and pants, while most of the women dressed in camisole tops and light pieces of brightly printed cloth wrapped around their waists. A display of aluminum pots, pans, and cups made from melted down pop cans drew a good crowd. I cringed at the thought that people might be using the toxic aluminum pots for cooking.

Most of the people around Majunga are descendants of the Bantus who migrated about one thousand years ago, mixed with the blood of European and Arabian traders and sailors. Though the Bantus formed the first kingdom in Madagascar, it did not survive well after the founders died and subsequent generations broke into small tribal groups. The Merina kingdom in the highlands easily subdued the Bantus, resulting in the Bantus' second-class status that still exists hundreds of years later.

After we strolled through the market, we climbed aboard a small motorboat for a ride across Bombetoka Bay at the mouth of the Betsiboca River. Our primary target bird for the day was a Malagasy Kingfisher. These birds live at the edge of a mangrove forest across the bay. I had seen kingfishers that fish from low hanging vegetation near streams. A bird waits in the reeds that grow between the forest and the slow moving river and when a small fish swims past him, he flies up and dives into the water to catch the fish. The kingfisher returns to the reed, carefully aligns the fish in its beak and swallows it whole. Mark told us that the color on the malachite was an unbelievably intense blue. My kind of bird! I couldn't wait.

Mangrove trees are of medium height and grow along saline shores in the tropics and subtropics.

Healthy mangroves serve as nurseries for certain types of fish. The young can feed safely within the complex tree roots and branches underwater until they are large enough to move out into the sea. With little air movement in the mangrove forests, the humidity is extremely high, creating yet another special environment that supports unique wildlife like certain species of mollusks, crabs, turtles, and other small creatures that become food for birds. The mangrove roots also slow down incoming silt-bearing water, causing the soil to build up and create new land. Later, the roots in the new soil guard against land erosion, protecting fragile coastal areas. Unfortunately, mangrove trees have been harvested for lumber in many places, exposing the shore to erosion and threatening villages and farmland with saltwater inundation.

Crossing the bay, we motored past a family wedged into their narrow dugout, carved out of a tree trunk. The family seemed to be on their way to one of the nearby islands. The father paddled the boat in the stern, and the mother and children sat quietly, one in front of the other, on the floor of the slim craft. One child hung his arm over the side and dragged his fingers in the water, watching the ripples flow back as their boat moved forward. Although it was 2004, it could have easily been 500 years earlier as I watched this timeless scene of a family serenely cross the water in an ancient form of transportation.

As we neared the mangrove forest, our motorman turned off the engine when we were still thirty feet from reeds that grew out into the bay. We drifted toward the mangroves with only bright licks of water brushing against the hull to break the silence.

"There it is," Mark whispered, pointing toward a bright metallic-blue bird about five-inches long, the Malagasy kingfisher. The kingfisher's tiny feet gripped a thin reed and swayed in the light breeze, giving us a great opportunity to observe the dazzling blue of his back and his reddish-brown chest, speckled head, and long black bill. The bird had no interest in us but watched the water for ripples that might indicate something tasty below. No fish swam by as we watched, so although there was no drama, it certainly was a stunning little bird.

To our delight, we also found a Madagascar Sacred Ibis, which has a white body with a black head, legs, and rump feathers, and the long, curved, ibis bill good for poking in soft river bottoms. Any bird with Madagascar in its name is found only, or almost only, in Madagascar. As I carefully observed this brilliant-colored bird, I kept telling myself, *Take a good look— unless you plan to return.*

The first full day observing wildlife in Madagascar was relaxing, and we all looked forward to three more weeks of exploring this fascinating and diverse island country.

Arab-style dhow, *near Majunga*
on the north coast of Madagascar

CHAPTER 2

Ankarafantsike National Park

Our three a.m. wake-up call the next morning came all too early. Mark had arranged for passable breakfast snacks for the bus ride, and most important, coffee. We drove inland from Majunga about 64 miles southeast toward Ankarafantsike National Park.

Before humans inhabited Madagascar, tropical dry forests dominated the northwestern coast and inland for several hundred miles. However, civilization has destroyed 97 percent of these forests. In an attempt to save the last remaining section of dense, dry deciduous forest in Madagascar, the government designated this shrinking area a national park in 2002. The dry season in the tropical forests ends in October, so most of the tall thin trees and sparse understory were leafless during our October visit, leaving the bare ground exposed to the harsh sun.

Umbrella Birds & More

When we arrived at the park, I noticed six back-packing tents set up under a grass roof over a concrete pad near the parking lot. The tents were so close together everyone would know if someone turned over. These tents were the extent of tourist accommodations at the park. For people like us, we wanted a bit more comfort, thus the early three-hour drive. Since our visit, the government has built better accommodations at the park allowing birders to arise fully rested for dawn bush walks.

My favorite bird that day was the Black Egret, a medium-sized wading bird that feeds in groups along the shore of the park's fresh-water lake. On the hunt, they spread their wings around their heads to shade the water. Fish are attracted to the shade, making them easy targets for the hungry birds. This is called canopy feeding. At first, the egrets looked like several black umbrellas opened, but abandoned, at the water's edge. In an instant, one umbrella became an egret with a long neck and legs. Then another unwrapped himself and then another. The egrets walked a few paces and with a swish became umbrellas again. The black egrets assume this position so quickly that it is difficult to see the transition. I have seen that same graceful movement in modern dance performances, the dancer bent forward, arms gracefully forming an arc overhead. *Could some choreographer have seen one of these birds?*

More than a decade later, I still chuckle when I recall that day. During the first days of any birding trip, there are so many new birds to see, it is easy to get overwhelmed. Even now, with more than fifteen years experience as a birder, my head still spins with the abundance of birds and wildlife in a new place. Looking back, I remember the moment in Ankarafantsike National Park when Mark pointed to the right side of a large bush and said, "Look at the bird over here! This is a difficult bird to see, so catch a glimpse now! We will see lots of those other birds later!"

I don't think many of us knew enough to take Mark's advice. At the time Mark said this, I thought, *But the ones over here are prettier!*

On that particular day, the bird Mark wanted us to see was a Vanga, a name that stuck in my head as a new family of birds to me. It could have been the Van Dam's Vanga, truly a difficult bird to find and the reason for Mark's excitement—someone who is generally quiet and subdued. He kept a list of what we saw and the Van Dam's vanga was on the list. I glanced at the vanga, white and grey, but not as eye catching as the other birds, so I returned to observing them. We saw a lot of vangas on the trip, but never another one of that species.

Numerous times I have thought about that lesson and now, I always pay attention to the guide's judgment of where my focus should be, even giving up some lovely eye candy for a plainer but rarer bird. At that point in my birding career I did not understand the importance of the "personal bird list" to some birders, so I just absorbed with pleasure the birds I saw. I don't regret that. Now that I do keep a list, I don't take it too seriously like some birders who have a celebration for every milestone, though I don't mind the libations that accompany someone else's party.

We saw the Madagascar Crested Ibis with its rusty brown body, a red face, a black crest, and the curved ibis bill. We also saw White-breasted Mesite, Coquerel's Coua, Red-capped Coua, and a Squacco Heron. I loved that name right away. This heron is stocky with a short fluffy neck, a thick body, and a buffy-brown back. I've seen squacco herons several times since, and they always make me smile. Some bird names just make the bird all the more special.

My First Lemurs

I went to Madagascar to observe lemurs as well as birds. While at the park, I got my first glimpses of lemurs—*ever*. At a frustrating distance, we saw a few lemurs called Coquerel's Safika and a troop of Brown Lemurs, but not close enough for me to enjoy. However, these were my first lemurs, worth a cheer even at the distance. At that point, the nuances among the lemur species were lost on me but they were lemurs, and that was exciting. After that, I kept telling myself, *I saw lemurs*! I wanted more, and Mark assured us, we would see plenty of lemurs, and up close.

By the end of our visit at Ankarafantsike National Park, I felt too overwhelmed with the abundance of wildlife encounters to absorb the finer points of all the new animals and birds. By any count, I certainly enjoyed that fabulous day. What a start to the trip!

How to Grow Rice

On our return trip from the national park back to Majunga, we got our first daytime look at rice fields and farmers planting the tiny shoots in their flooded fields. The first settlers brought rice with them from Borneo and now rice is the staple of the Malagasy diet. Our driver pulled the bus over and we climbed off to watch the farmers. They all waded with effort through knee-deep water and muck as they went about their work.

After Rivo explained what the fieldworkers were doing, he asked the women in the closest field for permission to photograph them. They laughed and even posed for our cameras. The women were transplanting the chartreuse rice shoots grown from seed in the nearby nursery fields. In another field, a man skimmed a huge paddle over the flooded mud surface to level it for planting.

Rivo explained, "All the farmers in a village plant their rice at the same time so that when it matures, the hungry birds are dispersed among all the fields and no one farmer's crop is stripped. They keep the paddies wet until just before harvest to keep down weeds and to allow the plants to absorb the dissolved nutrients. Then they drain the fields and let the paddies sit for a few days for the soil to become firmer. After that, the farmers cut the rice near ground level and leave the roots in the earth to decay and nourish the next crop. They can grow one to three crops of rice a year."

During our rice growing conversation I learned that after harvesting several crops of rice, the soil could be used to make bricks, a process we watched at another location. The residual roots provide organic matter for the brick making and if needed, more straw can be worked into the mud. Workers mold bricks into the desired shape then leave them to dry on the field.

Once the bricks harden, the workers stack them loosely, up to eight feet high with spaces for air vents and a fire. After baking for two or three days, often using rice husks for fuel, villagers use the bricks to build the two- and three-story houses common in and around Tana (Antananarivo). When workers take the soil off the fields for bricks, it leaves only the laterite clay, which means the farmer must weigh the economic advantage of rice over bricks.

Farmers' fields surround their homes. Typically, the farm animals occupy the ground level of the home and the families live in the upper stories. There are few chimneys because people let the smoke from their cooking fires fill their houses to protect against mosquitoes. As a result, lung disease is a serious health problem for people living in these houses and medical care is poor in rural areas. However, the threat of malaria carried by the mosquitoes is more worrisome than lung cancer, a disease that may or may not be contracted after years of breathing smoke.

That day when we looked around the paddy-filled valley, I found it difficult to imagine that thick forests had ever covered those valleys, as it had before the first humans arrived.

Back at our motel, we prepared for our next day's journey. We would take a flight south the next morning to the absolute opposite end of Madagascar, Fort Dauphine.

Wattle houses typical in southwest Madagascar

CHAPTER 3

Southern Madagascar and the Lemurs

After one more night in Majunga, we were back on the plane headed for Fort Dauphin, 620 miles to the southeastern coast of Madagascar. Three days at Berenty Wildlife Reserve promised a good dose of lemurs habituated to people, plus an introduction to birds of the dry southern climate.

When we changed planes in Tana, the common name for Antananarivo where we first landed in the central highlands, I noticed that green rice paddies filled the bottomlands in the middle of the city. Small rectangular houses built with the traditional mud bricks, some two or three stories tall, climbed the steep hillsides. The more modern and taller buildings constructed of concrete, clustered in one lowland area. Together, all of these structures accommodated a population of nearly one-and-a-half million people.

In contrast, my heart broke as we flew over hundreds of miles of barren red clay, the result of extreme deforestation. In Madagascar as in many tropical countries, the tropical forest soil is nutrient-poor to begin with and when humans cut down the trees and plant crops, the soil's limited fertility is depleted after only a few years. The Malagasies call this slash-and-burn agriculture *tavy* and it is the primary cause of the naked red soil. When farmers plow these thin soils, the under soil is exposed to the hot sun and releases the soil's organic matter as CO_2, which contributes to global warming.

Before long, the soil's surface becomes so hard that any rain runs right off, eroding the land and flowing into the sea. There is not enough time to change the traditional ways of farming in a country whose population has increased fourfold in the past 50 years. Rebuilding the soil is possible due to new technologies emerging but the process is slow.

From the air, I could see that the further south we traveled the land grew drier and gray scrub replaced the few scattered fields planted in the creases of the ruined mounds of red soil. This was the environmental collapse I feared I would witness—and experiencing it was sickening.

Fort Dauphin

As we neared the end of our two-hour flight from Tana, I could see the Indian Ocean, an indicator that we were close to Fort Dauphin, the southern most town in Madagascar. In 2004, Fort Dauphin had about 43,000 residents.

In 1648, Erienne de Flacourt of the French East India Company arrived in Fort Dauphin to quell discontent among the French soldiers posted there. He was the first naturalist to record sightings of many plant and animal species in Madagascar that are now extinct. The ten-foot-tall bird that de Flacourt called the "elephant bird" fascinated him. This flightless bird roamed the land near Fort Dauphin, weighed up to 1,100 pounds, and laid 20-pound eggs! Unfortunately, the local people hunted the large and slow elephant bird to extinction.

De Flacourt also described many lemurs, some of which still live in southern Madagascar. When I read some of his accounts, I couldn't wait to see my first lemurs up close—an animal that immediately captured my imagination as a youngster when I first learned about them in *National Geographic.*

The plane swung over the brilliant turquoise water of the Indian Ocean and turned back toward the land. We descended and glided over the pristine beach. Just as the runway zipped under us the plane's engines revved up and the plane pulled up to regain altitude. My heart jumped and my blood pressure must've shot up. *Yikes! What's going on here?* I wondered.

The plane was a middle-aged Boeing 737 with six seats across, common on commuter routes at home, but not an aircraft I would expect to be doing aerial acrobatics. The plane skirted the blocky hills, turned back toward the ocean, and repeated the approach. This time I noticed a rusty ship carcass balanced on the offshore reef. As it turned out, I saw it on the third pass as well. The Malagasies on the flight chuckled indulgently when the plane's wheels finally smacked down on the runway and the plane bounced to a stop. Apparently, this was a familiar occurrence for them.

Outside the terminal, the uniformed airline crew gathered around a man much younger than the rest, also in uniform and wearing a sheepish smile. The older men took turns slapping the young pilot on the back and shaking his hand. I wondered, *How many more of our planes will be piloted by trainees?*

A Roadside Glimpse of Life

During the four-hour drive west to our next birding site, the Berenty Private Reserve, we had the opportunity to see how people lived in the spiny forest region in the arid southeastern third of Madagascar. We passed small houses made of thumb-sized strips of wood, sometimes finished with mud. Inside I could see a bed, a small fire ring for the evening smudge fire, and an occasional shelf in the shadows. In the intense heat, I imagined the mud-covered houses had to be stifling inside. The structures seemed tiny until we saw how much of the family and village life took place outside. There were times I felt as if we were driving through someone's home because the outdoor scenes were so intimate: a man sitting on the ground and playing with his toddlers; a young woman bathing in a water trough dressed only in a light wrap; a woman sweeping her dirt yard with a handful of twigs. Outside one home, a small charcoal cooker supporting a bubbling rice pot sat on the bare earth.

Everywhere, women and girls carried water from the river or the roadside water taps, each container appropriate for the size of the bearer. *No need for books on their heads to teach posture here,* I mused. A few younger women strolled around with a paste of manioc flour on their faces for sun-protection. It reminded me of mudpacks women in the United States use for moisturizing their skin.

We stopped next to a wide riverbed where women filled their water containers and washed their clothes in the ankle deep water. People carrying loads on their heads or pushing bikes meandered across the two-lane bridge. We had to let our little blue bus cross the bridge without us because the approach had crumbled and looked rather dangerous. Once we all got off the bus, the driver urged the reluctant vehicle up six-inch steps to the bridge itself, mindful to protect the underbody with each lurch. To my relief, he made it across the bridge safely with the bus still intact.

Several tombs next to the road reminded me of the ones we had seen at Royal Hill. Chest-high plastered walls surrounded a central space where a small structure with a sloped roof held the ancestor. Rocks often filled the courtyard around the tomb. From the road, we could see figures and symbols that celebrate the deceased's life painted on the white walls. Though traditional practices differ in some ways from those we saw in the highlands near Antananarivo, people here also build the tombs near their homes and villages, believing the spirits of their ancestors can guide descendants' lives. The permanence of the tombs made clear the strong link the Malagasy people feel for their land. It would be difficult for them to consider leaving their ancestral lands should environmental or economic changes become dire.

On some tombs zebu skulls with elegant horns rested on top to honor the ancestor's status. Zebus are a species of cattle that originated in India and spread across to the east coast of Africa. Other common names for zebu include humped cattle or Brahman. Researchers believe the first cattle were shipped to Madagascar from the east coast of Africa. These animals are well adapted to a hot, dry climate, although some varieties also do well in the rainforest.

The Malagasy people consider zebus a form of wealth. The more zebus a man owns, the higher his status, and it is the number of zebus, not their condition, that is important. Sadly, we saw many scrawny zebus desperately searching for a blade of grass on the stark landscape that they themselves created.

Zebus are used as sacred food for the feasts that mark major life passages and are often used as ceremonial gifts and religious sacrifices. Traditionally, when a wealthy owner of a zebu herd dies, all of the owner's animals, sometimes numbering in the hundreds, are killed for the feast. The family of the deceased saves the finest skulls for the tomb. Recently, as more Malagasies have been converting to Christianity, fewer zebus have been killed for the funeral feast—at least not the whole herd.

We approached our destination, Berenty Reserve, and my excitement rose. I was about to realize another lifetime dream of observing lemurs firsthand in their natural habitats. When we drove under the sign that said Berenty Reserve Naturelle H. A. H., I scanned the trees and shrubs that lined the road for lemurs. I knew they were close.

Ring-tailed Lemur, Berenty

CHAPTER 4

Among the Lemurs

My initial search for lemurs went unrewarded when we first drove into Berenty Private Reserve. Later, I learned that lemurs like certain vegetation for protection and food, and they have routes and territories that do not include the drive into the reserve. However, when we stepped off our bus into the magical world of Berenty Private Reserve, we discovered Ring-tailed Lemurs everywhere! They wandered around the private reserve and its small collection of buildings and open-air dining facilities, as well as around the bungalows where we stayed. Unabashed, the lemurs were going about their business without a care, almost oblivious to our human presence. Awed by the sight of lemurs, I just stood still and drank it all in. My impulse to hug one passed quickly—fortunately for me and for the lemur passing by me in that moment.

I almost couldn't believe we were there in the middle of this incredible place. The Berenty Private Reserve receives worldwide publicity for the owners' efforts to preserve lemurs and all the wildlife that lives in the same environment. The part of the Berenty plantation we would explore for the next three days is located along the Mandrare River, about 75 miles inland from the southern coast of Madagascar. The vegetation is a gallery forest, a type of forest that forms along a river or other body of water where, without the water, there are few trees. Surrounding this habitat is the spiny forest of southern Madagascar, which we would see more of when we traveled further north.

Berenty Reserve is part of a 2,500-acre concession granted to the de Heaulme family in 1936 for sisal hemp production at a time when sisal fiber was still used for ropes. Years ago, the family recognized the amazing diversity of wildlife on the land they owned and eventually dedicated 1,500 acres as a preserve where scientists and tourists are welcomed. The de Heaulme family's story is well recorded in *Lords and Lemurs,* a delightful book by Alison Jolly, a zoologist who studied the Berenty lemurs for 25 years.

Scientists have worked at Berenty since the 1960s, so the lemurs are well habituated to people. The 101 remaining species and subspecies of lemurs are descendants of the same pre-primate as monkeys. Lemurs range in size from the 25-gram Pygmy Lemur to the 25-pound Indri Lemur. They survive by adapting over time to ecological niches filled by other wildlife living outside of Madagascar. As an example of the niche specificity of lemurs, the small nocturnal lemur called the Aye-Aye lives in rainforests and uses a long, slender, middle finger to dig out grubs and small insects deep in the bark of trees, similar to what woodpeckers do in other ecosystems. Bamboo lemurs eat cyanide-laced bamboo, a niche filled by pandas in China. Learning about these lemurs' amazing adaptations was fascinating, and I hoped to see some of those particular lemurs during our tour.

The "Dancing" Lemurs

With Mark's promise of more lemurs and birds, I pulled myself away from the magnetic presence of the ring-tailed lemurs, found my bungalow, and tossed my bag inside. Then I joined the others in my tour group for a walk along a ten-foot-wide cattle trail lined with prickly brush, tamarind, and eucalyptus trees.

Before long, we heard the vigorous rustle of leaves to the side of the path. Then something started jerking bushes from side to side. Peering into the dry underbrush, we hoped to see another kind of Berenty lemur. We were not disappointed. A slim white animal the size of a small cat burst from the ground-level shrubs and galloped onto the path on springy hind legs with long arms waving. She had a baby glued to her back. The lemur paused in the path's center and her bright yellow eyes widened as she scanned the area, pricking her ears, alert for predators.

We stood perfectly still fascinated by this lemur and her baby. My body tingled as I stared, unable to even blink. *They were so close!*

The mother lemur looked our way and then back to the brush behind her. She made a quick series of *tsk, tsk, tsk* sounds to her family and then romped across the path and up a tree. Grasping the trunk with her hands and her powerful hand-shaped feet, the lemur shinnied rapidly into the protection of the limbs and leaves. In quick succession, five more adult Sifaka Lemurs bounced and flailed across the open ground and leapt into the same tree, expertly climbing the trunks and moving along tree branches to join the lead lemur and her baby in the canopy's safety.

After the lemurs disappeared, Mark explained that a natural predator of lemurs is the Fossa, a cat-like carnivore endemic to Madagascar. Fossas are compared to small cougars and they can climb up and down trees, as well as jump from tree to tree as the lemurs do. Fossas live in the Berenty Preserve along with the lemurs and this is one of the last places on earth where the fossa, an aggressive and solitary predator, can be found. About 50 percent of the fossa's food is lemurs—and the lemurs know it.

We later learned the cat-like lemur we saw is called Verreaux's Sifaka. These lemurs are fuzzy and mostly white with black, heart-shaped faces, black hands and feet, and a brown cap with a white brow band. Their black-tufted ears prick forward when curious or back when threatened. Tourists find them to be one of the most charming of the lemurs, and humans feel compelled, as we were, to photograph them because they are so animated, waving their arms and springing lightly with an effortless bounce. Tourists call them the "dancing lemurs" of Berenty, but these lemurs do not dance as we understand that term. To our delight, they use this bouncy gallop to move across open ground when they are out of their comfort zone high in the trees.

We found that photographing these lemurs "dancing" was easy. When we saw one in motion, we could prepare our cameras because we knew more would follow. These lemurs move quickly across potentially dangerous stretches of open ground. Verreaux's sifaka lemurs live in family groups of four to eight individuals. The dominant female leads the group on a daily route through the 64-foot-high tamarind canopy, searching for tasty leaves until naptime. When a road or a roof breaks the forest's canopy, she will lead the troop at full speed across the open space to the next safe tree, which is what we observed.

At the end of our first day observing several Verreaux's sifakas bounce across our path, we were inspired to try to emulate their wild thrashing movements. We laughed a lot in our attempts, but sadly, our human bodies were too heavy and our legs not springy enough to even approximate the lemurs' leaping grace.

Birds, Of Course!

Everywhere we explored in the reserve we observed so many birds—new to all of us—as they flew, strolled, and perched. Along a shaded trail by a small gully, I climbed the few steps up the bank to come face-to-face with a Madagascar (Malagasy) Paradise Flycatcher. His sky-blue eye-ring and fluttering white tail feathers, as long again as his seven-inch body, made a profound impression on me, as the first sighting of a particular species will do. We also spotted a Madagascar Sandgrouse, a Madagascar Cuckoo-hawk, and a Hook-billed Vanga. After dismissing the other vanga at Ankarafantsike National Park south of Majunga, I made a point of carefully studying the hook-billed vanga, even though it was a different species and a more common one.

Ringtails on the Trail

On another Berenty plantation path, we heard a meow sound from the bushes. A young ring-tailed lemur sat alone on a branch, which Mark said was an unusual sight. The lemur had yet to develop adult coloring except for his tail, which was barred like a raccoon's tail. We looked around for his family but the trees were quiet. He seemed to be pleading, perhaps calling for his mother, and meowed again. We approached, our cameras clicking. His eyes widened as he looked frantically from us to the trees and back. When we got too close, the youth warned us off with a little growl, then turned and scampered up the tree limb into the forest's canopy where we then heard the rustling of a larger animal.

Ring-tailed lemurs are one of the more familiar lemur species at Berenty and are affectionately called ringtails by the staff and scientists who study them. These lemurs look like slim raccoons, gray with black masks, and ringed tails that are not as fluffy as a raccoon's. Early the first morning, we found a family of ringtails sitting in the path with their white bellies exposed to the warmth of the rising sun. Their legs were splayed, arms limp at their sides, eyes drooping. Though languid, they were alert. At the slightest sound of a foot-scrape, their eyes snapped open and they dashed off to a safe tree.

Every day at Berenty we watched troops of ring-tails swagger along the roads, their rumps held high over extra-long hind legs. It all looked rather rude if they were walking away from us, which they usually were, but the gay wave of their long tails jerking side-to-side with each step was a delightful statement of their ease in their environment and proof enough of their benign attitude toward us.

Male ring-tailed lemurs engage in what are called stink fights to ward off potential rivals. We watched several males stroking their tails over their wrists where one of the stink glands is located, ready to wave them in the air and release their scent to threaten their opponents. A male will mark his territory by backing up to a branch or tree trunk, tail erect, and rub the branch with another scent gland located at the base of the tail. A female will do the same when she is in estrous and looking for a mate, and the male will rub his scent over the top of hers to mask it from other males.

We stayed for three days at Berenty where the ringtails were tame to the point of being pesky. They lurked in the rafters over the open-air dining area, waiting for a chance to swoop down and snatch whatever food had been left unguarded. With new visitors arriving every day, they had many opportunities to grab a snack. The staff discouraged that behavior because the bread they often managed to grab is not a nourishing diet for lemurs. Rivo coached us on lemur protocol in the dining area so we remained vigilant.

During a post-lunch break, I heard a yell from the cabin next to mine.

"What is it? Are you OK?" I yelled over.

"A lemur was in my cabin—right inside!" someone said. "It grabbed my banana. I guess I shouldn't have left the windows open, but it's so warm I just had to."

"Put away anything else they might find interesting, or you'll have another lemur in there," I warned.

I had just closed my eyes for a quick snooze when I heard a loud crash from the direction of another cabin, followed by light galloping sounds and then someone swearing. I looked over to see a troop of ringtails galumphing along the tin roof, single file, tails high, and hands waving. The lead lemur jumped for the limb of a tree and they all followed. Tree or roof—it all looks the same to a lemur. Fortunately, their route did not include my cabin so I could delight in the action without as much disturbance.

I loved Berenty Reserve, but we had more of Madagascar to see. Besides, I asked myself, *How could it get any better?*

I would soon find out.

Verreaux's Safika Lemur at Berenty, southern Madagascar

Harriet under a baobab tree in the spiny forest near Ifaty

CHAPTER 5

The Spiny Forest of Southwest Madagascar

After retracing the rough four-hour drive from Berenty back to Fort Dauphin, we took an hour flight to the northwest coastal town of Tulear. The spiny forest and its unique birds awaited us near the coastal village of Ifaty, another hour north by bus. Both towns are located on the eastern shore of Madagascar about 500 miles across the Mozambique Channel from Africa. Ifaty is a dusty fishing village that caters to tourists who want to lie in the sun and snorkel on the reefs. We stayed at one of those nice resorts right on the beach, but had little time for the leisure life.

The Sacred Spiny Forests

Our destination that day was the spiny forest, which is a vast desert forest that stretches around southwestern Madagascar. This unique area is also known as spiny thickets that the World Wildlife Fund (WWF) reports "receives only 12 to 24 inches of rain per year, yet is one of the most biologically significant places on Earth." The vegetation has adapted to the extremely dry weather and poor soil with plants producing small leathery leaves that preserve moisture and spines to discourage grazing animals.

Indigenous communities in the spiny forest revere their sacred forests and had kept them largely intact until recent times. Traditional practices included taboos on cutting trees in designated areas. For eons, the people lived off the land using tavy, the slash and burn agriculture. Land not designated as taboo was available to anyone who needed to use it and there was no need for cash.

As the population grew, eventually the free land could no longer support the needs of the people. They needed money to buy what they could not grow. The only way for people who live in the spiny forest to generate cash is to sell charcoal. Where the needs of the people have put pressure on sacred lands, reserves, and parks, the communities have had to relax customary taboos, which threatens the remaining trees and all the wildlife that have sought refuge on the sacred land.

In the 1960s, several international conservation organizations came together to work with Madagascar's government to address the pressure on natural resources. They surveyed what protected areas still existed in the spiny forest and the rest of the country. By the time we visited in 2004, conservationists were working with the communities to preserve the forest's habitats and wildlife.

On our first morning of birding in the spiny forest, I was eager to explore another brand new habitat.

I dressed in my lightest gear, long shirtsleeves and pants, a broad-brimmed hat, and sunblock. We ate early and headed out to our first birding spot before the heat increased, knowing it would be ferocious.

Sacrificing the Environment for Charcoal

Our small bus turned onto a road that ended in a cluster of mud and wattle houses. Several men jumped up from under the eaves of the nearest house led by a Rastafarian-looking fellow. "Don't worry," Mark assured us. "Mosa isn't as fierce as he appears."

Mosa greeted Mark with a big smile, a firm handshake, and a manly hug, and then introduced the six guides with him. We shook hands all around, then broke into two groups; one for the avid birders and one for the generalists and those interested in photos and plant life as well as birds. I joined the birdy group.

As we followed our local guide, Tov, into the scrub, two other guides disappeared ahead of us, trotting along the sandy paths that vehicles had carved into the dry bush. We passed a shallow pit strewn with tiny bits of charcoal. These pits looked like the charcoal pits I saw in Tanzania in the 1960s when I taught school during my Peace Corps work. I never knew the exact details of making charcoal, but I recognized the pits.

When I asked Tov about the pit, he gave a deep sigh. "Yes, villagers chopped down one of the few remaining hardwood trees to make charcoal.." Then he explained the process. "They bury the wood, cover it with the sandy soil, and set it afire. When they do that, smoke billows out from the mound of wood and soil. It doesn't burn all the way like in a cooking fire, but just enough to leave charcoal. Then they put the charcoal in a large bag, as tall as me, and sell each bag for one dollar."

We had driven past the piles of bags sitting by the side of the road that morning. "If they can get a cart," added Tov, "they will take them to the market in Ifaty."

Most of the few remaining trees that we could see were isolated baobabs scattered amidst the scrub. In the arid environment these trees store water in their fat swollen trunks. They can grow up to 36 feet in diameter and are topped with absurdly tiny tops. Six species of baobabs grow in Madagascar, while only one species populates all of Africa. The baobob trees I saw in Tanzania and Kenya were not the same species we were seeing in Madagascar.

Baobabs are not good for making charcoal, so perhaps this is why some were still standing. Baobab leaves have a medicinal use, the fruit is edible, and the tough seeds of the fuzzy fruit yield cooking oil. When the inevitable droughts descend on the spiny desert, starving people will eat the baobab's leaves and shoots, as well as the meager pulp around the seeds. In the worst drought, trees are chopped down to let the thirsty cattle chew on the pulpy interior.

As we continued down the soft sand road, Tov pointed out the endemic plants called euphorbias that are full of spines and tiny leaves. The octopus plant, didiera, reminded me of ocotillos in the southwest deserts of the United States. The tall clumps of branches can grow 45-feet tall and have long, vicious spines. The small leathery leaves conserve water and were found on similar plants that seemed bare from a distance. Later, Mark told us that the Tandroy who live in the area use the thin pieces of hard wood from these plants for fences and the walls to their houses.

The widely spaced bushes and trees gave little shade as we walked, and as the sun rose the heat seared us through our clothing. Walking in the deep sand was hard work and I veered to the edges of the narrowing road, trying to find solid ground. It seemed the plants had the same idea and I got stabbed several times when I ventured too close to their territory.

In Pursuit of a Splendid Bird

We strolled through the gray-green bushes identifying common birds and plants until we heard a whistle and a shout in the distance. "Follow me, he has found one," Tov whispered as he waved for us to follow.

Found what? I wondered. *Something good I hope— from the way he's running, it sure looks like it!*

For ten minutes, we mushed through the soft sand, legs aching and wilting in the heat. Finally, we caught up to Tov. He signaled us to stop, wait, and be quiet. He pointed to the path ahead. Still panting, we heard tiny crisp cracks from the brush on the right side of the path. The two guides who had run ahead of us slowly walked in our direction through the bare grey stalks. We peered into the brush, tense with anticipation.

"Look, look," Tov whispered, pointing in front of the other guides.

A slender, leggy, blue-gray bird with a rusty breast and the size of a chicken picked its way through the thorny branches. He stopped at the edge of the brush and then stepped on to the open pathway.

Tov whispered again, "Olive-capped Coua." (Pronounced "koo-a".) We focused our binoculars and marveled at every detail. Like all couas, this bird had a large and striking bright blue, featherless eye patch. The rusty cap on this particular bird's head identified it as the Olive-capped Coua, one of many strange anomalies I discovered in the bird-naming world. Whether the cap was rusty or olive colored, the bird was gorgeous. It leisurely walked across the path, stepped into the brush on the far side, and disappeared. We lowered our binoculars, exhaled, and smiled.

Shells for Sale

During our afternoon rest time when birds were quiet, I wandered along the beach in shaded areas protected against the fierce sun. A group of women crouched just past the beach property line and displayed their offerings on portable tables; bright clam shells, shiny brown cowries the size of my fist, and patterned cone shells that had to have been taken off the reef when the animal was alive. As a scuba diver, I understand the temptation to take live shells. They have stunning patterns and are clean and shiny because the animal inside covers the shell with its flesh when it is relaxed and feeding. However,

I worry when I see these pristine shells for sale, knowing how the removal and trade in such shells can upset the ecosystem. The reef along the coast is lengthy and only a few people are harvesting the shells, so I thought, *The Madagascar shell populations are sustainable—for now.*

When I saw the enterprising women displaying their shells, hoping to make a day's wages, I decided to be optimistic and give them the benefit of the doubt. I told myself, *One positive way to think about the shell trade is that it brings in cash, which might buy food, and perhaps spare the remaining trees in the forests—a tough choice.*

Then I considered the other side of the situation: *Maybe I shouldn't buy anything. It may also be a bad precedent to encourage the shell trade.*

Wanting to support the local economy and protect the local environment as well, I wondered, *How will the reef populations be sustained as tourist trade increases?* I didn't have a clear answer for myself on the beach that day and I still don't know the answer more than a decade later. In the end, I did not buy any shells.

In the late afternoon, only David and I chose to go out birding again. The merciless sun proved the point about the wisdom of birding early. We knew the chances of seeing something were slim, but you never know. The others chose to read, or sit under an umbrella on the beach, or nap. For a few moments as I struggled through the soft sand, feeling my hot shirt ruffling on my sweaty skin, I knew what ever we saw, I would remember the experience forever.

Some of my group in Isalo National Park,
south central Madagascar.

CHAPTER 6

On the Road to Isalo

After leaving the spiny forest, we had a couple of long drives ahead of us before reaching Ranomafana National Park on the eastern coast of Madagascar. Along the way, Mark had several interesting stops planned to break the trip into manageable stretches.

On the ninth day of our trip, we left Ifaty to drive north and east on the only road up the center of the island toward Ranomafana. Our first day on the road proved to be the longest leg, 585 miles to Isalo National Park, where we spent the night. On later birding trips, I found out a drive of this length was not unusual in the many countries where rare birds lived and Madagascar was a prime example.

Light traffic on the paved, two-lane road allowed us time to observe the oncoming vehicles on their way south, every vehicle jammed with passengers and cargo. Trucks hauled bags of charcoal, grain sacks, boxes, fuel, and people, while pickups and smaller vehicles carried cargo and passengers, with some people hanging off the sides. Our bus was possibly the lightest vehicle on the road and passed the others easily, sometimes on a curve, and always exciting. When our small bus approached trucks that swerved side to side with no centerline to guide them, I tried to reassure myself that I had survived similar hazards in Tanzania and Malawi. I was afraid to look over the driver's shoulder at the speedometer, but I did fasten my seat belt hoping it would actually hold me tight if we went off the road!

Madagascar Partridges

We stopped occasionally to stretch and eat, but even so, it was a long day on the bus. Fortunately, we had air conditioning for the hottest mid-day hours. Finally, we turned east off the main road and picked up a local guide in Ranohira, a requirement for the visit to nearby Isalo National Park. This park is known for its deep canyons, dramatic sandstone formations, and gorgeous stretches of grassy savannahs. For us birders, it was a chance to see the Madagascar Partridge, which is only found in subtropical areas of Madagascar.

In the later afternoon, we welcomed the short climb up one of the sculpted buttes to reach the spot where the partridges might appear at dusk. The chance to stretch my muscles and breathe deeply felt divine after a day of sitting on the bus. We enjoyed the view on the ridge looking down on a grassy, flat, valley floor. The sun played on the dramatic sandstone formations that surrounded us and the shadows shifted on grey and beige rocky outcrops that popped into view. The day cooled as the sun reached for the horizon and we rested our tired eyes by studying the strange vegetation nearby. I loved the pachypodia, also called elephant's foot, a desert plant that resembles a fat gourd with several thick stems growing out of the top, each crowned with a sweet yellow flower. Aloe and other dusty green succulents squirted out of the crevices.

The five of us from Portland posed for a photo holding our hometown newspaper, *The Oregonian*. We planned to submit the photo to the newspaper's travel section when we returned to Portland. In the end, we didn't follow through, and I regret I didn't take at least one photo of all of us without the paper. However, I can still recall how serene I felt amidst peaceful wildlife surrounded by bizarre plants.

While we waited for the birds, a few of us sat on the exposed sandstone and soaked up the rocks' warmth, quietly trading stories of other desert visits. At one point, Mark called softly to us, "Don't move, but look under that overhanging rock. Madagascar partridges, one of our target birds for this location."

The low light highlighted the round little birds and we could see the brown back, white-striped grey belly, and the dark head. Across a dip in the rock and under a giant overhang, five of the fat Madagascar partridges walked back and forth as if looking for something; seeds, or a hole for shelter, or maybe a trail that evaded them. Finally, they fluffed their feathers and settled on the warm rock shelf as dark shadows crawled across the flat desert.

My First Lamba, Something to Shop For!

We stayed in new cabins that had been built for park visitors in an open area away from the rocks. As usual we retired early, but just before climbing into bed I went outside. Far from the cabin lights, I first checked the ground with my flashlight looking for insects. Then I planted my feet and tipped my head back to enjoy the stars, a favorite desert activity. I knew it was best to stargaze lying on my back, but I didn't know what might be waiting for me around my feet.

The night sky felt thick over my head, studded with thousands of pricks of light. The Milky Way flowed across the black dome and I picked out groups of stars that might have been constellations that I did not know. Gratitude flowed over me as I gazed at the boundless universe on a perfectly clear night, far from civilization.

After a comfortable night's sleep, once again we joined the northbound traffic on the main road. Two hours later we pulled off the road and walked a short distance into the scrubby brush of another new environment, this one with less rock and more desert, and home to several more birds.

We were standing on the edge of a deep sandy road, binoculars ready for the next birdcall, when a cart approached drawn by two jet-black zebus. The driver was a man wrapped in a dark red cloth imprinted with enormous yellow, blue, and green flowers. One glance and I loved this colorful wrap.

"Rivo, what do they call that fabulous colorful wrap that man has on?"

"It's a lamba. Very popular here."

"I want one!"

Rivo smiled at me indulgently, and did not reply.

I'll find one, I vowed to myself.

The cart passed and the woman and girl also riding in the cart along with several bags of charcoal, wore more subdued clothing. They waved and stood up so they could watch us as the zebu plodded on.

Learning a Bird Song in Malagasy

The long bus ride went on and on. Rivo suggested, "Since you are all birders, would you like to learn a song about a bird? It's one the children sing and it's about a kestrel. It is quite simple."

In our birding outings, we had seen several Madagascar Banded Kestrels sitting on sticks looking for lizards or other prey. Its relative, the American Kestrel, is a common raptor in North America. So, I loved the idea of learning a song about a familiar bird. Besides, I love to sing and always welcome the opportunity.

"It's in Malagasy," Rivo said. *Even more fun,* I thought.

He sang the song and I thought, *The melody is simple, but the words!* I wondered if I could ever figure them out. I have learned many songs through "oral tradition," meaning there is no written music. What you hear is what you must learn—and in an unfamiliar language. For me, hearing what is said is a real challenge. I did my best to listen, but finally I had to ask Rivo to spell the words.

This is what I wrote with strikes added to help me find the syllables:

man/dihi/za rah/hi/tsi/ki/tsi/ka (2 times)
hi/a/na/ra/nay (2 times)
man/dihi/za rah/hi/tsi/ki/tsi/ka
hi/a/na/ra/nay raha/fa/ra/ra/no
man/dihi/za man/dihi/za
man/dihi/za rah/hi/tsi/ki/tsi/ka

Then I wrote what I was hearing, which didn't look at all like what he spelled out: mandeeza ra-he-tzi-ki-tzi-ka hee/-a-na-ra-nai. I gave up, but I did finally learn some approximation of the song and loved having another language in my repertoire. More than a decade later, I can still sing this song although the occasions for doing so are rare.

While we struggled with this difficult song, our bus driver could hardly contain his choking laughter— our efforts sounded so funny to him.

I was reminded of my summer in Malawi years before. My Crossroads Africa group was constructing a building for the Young Pioneers who were being trained for leadership in the new nation. Their instructors, two Israelis, had them marching everywhere and singing as they went, which was a delightful background to our work. One day I heard a familiar tune, "Oh! Susanna," but I could not recognize the words. As I strained to listen, I finally picked out the heavily-accented phrase, "I'm going to see Kamuzu with my banjo on my knee." They were singing in English! "Kamuzu" was the name they called their new president, Hastings Kamuzu Banda. Since most of the trainees lived in rural areas and did not speak English well, if at all, their accents obscured the words. We were able to learn some of their songs, even though they were in the national language of Malawi, named Chinyanja at the time and later changed.

A few years after my Malawi summer, I met some college students visiting the United States from Malawi. In a friendly attempt to demonstrate my mastery of their language, I sang one of the songs I learned from the Young Pioneers. Their peals of laughter met my attempt, so, now, when I sing the song Rivo taught us in Madagascar, I imagine I sound just as mushy in my pronunciation as those Young Pioneers.

While eating lunch by the road that day, we heard one of the most uplifting birdcalls I have ever encountered. We had stopped on the eastern side of the highlands where increased rainfall nurtured thicker vegetation. Far over the forest canopy a pair of birds flew, looping, diving, and making a piercing, descending call that they repeated two or three times per swoop. They paused and then called again.

"Cuckoo-rollers," Mark noted.

The birds were just silhouettes against the sky, but their flight and joyful song grabbed everyone's attention. That was another moment that I will never forget. Over the course of several days, I heard the same sharp call, and to this day I delight remembering that carefree flight.

After many years of birding, I now look back and know that joy is too strong an attribute for birds.

They do what they do because it is in their genes—
but I do not deny the joy I feel while watching them.
Birds thrill me in so many ways. Sometimes a bird
has flamboyant colors, or its song touches my heart,
or perhaps I know I am observing a rarely seen bird.
That's why I go on birding trips—I treasure those
uplifting moments that make me smile.

Golden Bamboo Lemur watching Harriet,
Ranomafana National Park.

CHAPTER 7

Our First Rainforest, Ranomafana National Park

Driving north from Isalo National Park, the landscape changed from desert to lush green rice fields as we climbed into the highlands. After visiting a paper making craft shop in Fianaransoa in southeastern Madagascar, we continued another 33 miles to the Hotel Thermal in Ranomafana National Park, which was 168 miles south of Antananarivo.

Tourists are warned that much of Ranomafana National Park can only be seen by climbing many steep and muddy hillsides covered in thick tropical vegetation. I'm sure there were flat places, but I would soon learn there were days of climbing straight up and then descending, only to climb up again. I rather enjoyed the exercise, often lacking on birding tours, even though managing my body temperature was a challenge in the unfamiliar humidity. Mark arranged for a private guide for the one person in our group unable to cope with the steep trails. She saw a lot of what we did, and sometimes something else just as exciting. I appreciated the flexibility on our tour to adapt to particular people's physical restrictions and still show them interesting aspects of the country.

Wet, Wet, Wet

Ranomafana National Park was a rainforest at its wettest, so we always carried rain gear. In the heat, a poncho was a better cover than a sweaty jacket. Mark bought us umbrellas, which was the best idea because they provided good ventilation and rain protection. Most of the umbrellas were black but I quite liked my white one with purple spots. Fortunately for me, when we were after birds our umbrellas were down. I didn't know then that the color white might scare the birds away.

I was never tempted to just let the rain pelt down on me like some of my fellow travelers. Wet clothing felt uncomfortable long after the shower. Sweat might slowly evaporate, but after a heavy rain shower I felt wet and uncomfortable until we returned to the lodge and a dry set of clothes. Many times, I just turned off that feeling of discomfort and stayed focused on the birds and the experiences of being in Madagascar. Seeing a fabulous bird after great sacrifice made it all worthwhile. Other times, I just got grumpy.

Ranomafana National Park was established in 1991 and is one of Madagascar's newest rainforest parks, all of which are located on the eastern side of the island where tropical storms blow in from the Indian Ocean year round. More than 100 inches of rain fall annually on the island's eastern side and there is no real dry season, only periods of less rain. The climate is always humid and hot. Thick plants fill every layer of the forest from the ground up. A changing variety of vegetation and wildlife can be found at each level, all the way to the top of the canopy, which can be more than 200 feet high. The canopy of a rain forest is where the greatest amount of bird and animal activity occurs. Unfortunately for us, we couldn't see much of that rich environment, but we saw enough at ground level to make us happy.

The discovery of the Golden Bamboo Lemur in 1986 by Patricia C. Wright, Ph.D., a primatologist, anthropologist, and conservationist, spurred the government and the international foundations and organizations working to preserve Madagascar wildlife to formalize protection of what is now Ranomafana National Park. The Golden Bamboo Lemur was a strong indication of the area's diversity of wildlife, which is why it was essential for the area to be protected. We hoped to be so lucky as to see the golden bamboo lemur along with many of the eleven other lemur species living in the park. While we toured the park, I thought of Dr. Wright with much gratitude for the crucial environmental work she did in Madagascar.

Leeches

In an orientation on the park, we were told to watch out for leeches that lurk in the bushes. Let me first say that leeches get a bum rap. Compared to ticks, whose bites can make my flesh swell and

179

ache for days, leeches are innocuous when they feed, although I did not know that at the time. I read that Willi Unsoeld, a legendary mountaineer, had spent an unplanned night on the top of Mt. Everest and lost all but one toe to frostbite. After nine of his toes were amputated, the wounds on his feet got infected and swollen to the point of almost splitting the flesh. The medical solution in India was to attach leeches to his feet to suck out the fluids.

Willi proudly showed his foot with the one remaining toe, a little one, to me and the other Outward Bound Instructor trainees when he joined us for a few days in Oregon after my Peace Corps experience. I thought his sentimental attachment to that toe was sweet. After learning how the leeches had saved Willi's life, I thought, *How can anyone not at least respect the work that leeches can do?*

However, I admit it is quite revolting when leeches are discovered in the act—especially when you realize the leeches are sucking your blood. During our time in Madagascar, we tucked our pants into our socks and sprayed our lower legs and boots with repellant to protect against both leeches and mosquitoes. It worked quite well for me but some of my companions were not so lucky.

Our first morning in Ranomafana, the birdy group arose before dawn for our omelets and coffee, and then headed out for another birding trek. Seven of us climbed on the bus at 5:30 a.m., along with Mark and our local guide, taking a short ride up the gravel road that carries traffic between the highlands and the west coast in central Madagascar. It is barely wide enough for the heavily loaded trucks to pass, but at that hour we were alone. The small parking lot for Ranomafana National Park is located on a promontory overlooking a huge swath of dark jungle. From there, we watched as the dawn's light struggled to break through the overcast skies.

Before we began our hike, we were drawn to a fascinating collection of moths resting next to the porch light of the ranger's cabin. The largest moth was five inches across with furry tan wings. It clung to the wall, flaring its wings to expose the pink, red, and black, eye-shaped markings—no doubt presenting a fierce face to a predator.

After our moth observations, we followed Mark past a large map of the trails and plunged down the steep path through thick vegetation. Well-placed stairs slowed our slippery descent. We stopped to study a a tiny insect that Mark spotted on someone's pack strap. It was a Giraffe Beetle, and looked like a spotless ladybug with a very long, black beak protruding from the front of its body. While observing this strange insect I thought, *You never know what you might find in this odd place.*

Fifteen minutes later, we were at the valley floor where a footbridge spanned a boisterous river. We crossed and ascended again into the rainforest getting wet in a warm drizzle. Along the way, we tracked birds and lemurs. Around 11 a.m., we found the second group of birders—the late risers—waiting at an overlook, a wooden platform built on a ridge for viewing the valley below which, at that point, was filled with white clouds. The others were as wet as we were. While Ross Smith, a retired Australian doctor in our group, rested on a bench, I noticed that his pant legs had several watery red spots below the knees.

"So, what's with your legs?" I asked.

"Ah, just a few leeches," he answered, nonplussed. "I don't know why they stopped climbing at my knees, but they did and I'm glad of it! I guess they got their fill and left. The wounds kept bleeding for a while and messed up my pants though."

Ross and his wife, Lesley, were world travelers. They carried only one small suitcase apiece during the trip, and washed their clothes every day. I knew the spots must have annoyed him.

I looked down at my boots and legs with new interest. A long skinny critter was just diving into the mesh in my boot. I pulled it off and tried to flick it off my finger. The leech didn't flick. I wiped it off on an overhanging branch, hoping I injured it enough so it wouldn't bother anyone else. Satisfied, I turned my attention to other interests, like lunch, which the guides with the later group had brought for us all.

For the afternoon, the group split up again and about eight people followed a guide into the jungle to see a waterfall. I was tired and wet, and needed a break from the rainforest for a while, so I joined a few others returning to the hotel for an afternoon rest.

After the hike down to the river again and up the other side, we discovered our bus was not there, but an empty dump truck full of road workers had pulled over to let off some men. We asked the driver if he could take the five of us down the hill and he agreed, as is the custom in places with few vehicles. I clambered into the back followed by the others, ready to sit among the bags of cement and gravel. No sooner had I sat down then the truck's owner jumped out of the cab and invited me to join him inside with the other woman in our group. I was already settled so I declined. He seemed disappointed, maybe embarrassed, that a *vazaha,* (a white woman) would have to ride in the back of his vehicle. I considered briefly that he might think I was rude to refuse his offer—a possible cultural gaff—but from past experiences I knew that the workers would be more interesting to me than a polite conversation in a dry cab. Besides, I was already soaked and the rain had let up.

As the truck picked up speed, two men leaning against the back sang out the first line of a song. The rest of the men answered him. They sang all the way down the hill, reminding me of the call and response songs I had heard years ago at the Malawi youth camp. My decision to sit in the back with the workers was the right one for me! I really enjoyed listening to the workmen sing for their own pleasure. So often, songs I hear in another country are performances, but these men sang for the shear joy of singing. What a gift for me!

Back at the hotel I took a welcomed nap. Afterward, I heard a commotion outside; the hikers had returned. I leaned out my window and fellow travelers Nancy and Charles passed by my room. Blood spotted their clothing and I mentioned this.

"Oh yes, they found us," Nancy responded. "We stopped every ten minutes to pick them off one another, but we saw a lovely waterfall and had a very nice hike."

They plodded off to their room, leaving behind a blood-filled leech that inched its way along the cement walkway where they had been standing. Later, after discovering a spot of blood on the seat of my pants, I realized that at least one leech had found me tasty, too.

The terrestrial leeches we encountered in the rainforest are smaller than the aquatic Asian varieties and they look like hair-thin inchworms. They wait on the leaf tips, waving their fore-bodies, until a warm-blooded creature passes. Then they grab whatever they touch and inch their way upward until they find a warm, soft place to feed. Unless the leech is discovered while attached, it can finish its meal in half an hour and drop back into the jungle to digest the meal for the next four months, leaving a weeping wound on the host. I comforted myself with the knowledge that leeches do not carry any known diseases and are harmless—except to the host's psyche.

Two Rare Lemurs

Researchers estimate that there are only 1,000 Golden Bamboo Lemurs left in Madagascar and thus, on earth. Mark thought we had a good chance of seeing one that day, a rare opportunity and one I hoped we would experience!

We walked slowly through the rainforest single file, strung way out along a narrow path with big gaps between us. The birder ahead of me motioned to be quiet. He pointed toward a clump of thick bamboo, gnarly vines, and tough leaves on a variety of skinny trees that fill the space up into the canopy. Cracking and crunching came from that direction. At eye-level about fifteen feet away, a medium sized lemur chomped away on a shattered, three-inch stalk of bamboo. He had dense, grey-brown fur, darker on the head, a short muzzle, and fuzzy round ears. This one had white tufts on the tips of his ears, the field mark that differentiated this lemur from the other two bamboo lemurs. He had almost chewed the stem in two. Three strands of the tough outer wood kept the lower part of the stem from falling to the ground.

I looked across to my informant who mouthed to me, "Bamboo lemur." *Oh, my,* I thought, *another one of those once-in-a-lifetime moments. I need to study this little guy carefully.*

I've never figured out how to do that exactly, but the impulse to preserve the moment overcomes me at times like that. Years later, this scene is still clear in my mind. Of course, I got a little help remembering thanks to the photo taken by the other birder who caught the moment the lemur and I stared at one another, only about ten feet apart. The collar on the lemur's neck indicated that he was a study subject, wild but somewhat accustomed to people.

This had to be the Greater Bamboo Lemur, the largest of the bamboo lemurs, weighing up to five pounds. Of course, he was eating his favorite food, a type of bamboo, although the greater bamboo lemur will occasionally eat flowers, fungi, and fruit. As I watched this lemur calmly munching away on a plant that is toxic to every other animal because of its cyanide content, I thought, *What a sweet animal. And what a tough digestive system he must have.*

In a day, this lemur eats enough cyanide in his bamboo meals to kill twelve animals of the same size. This particular lemur's belly was large and swollen, and I wondered if this was a pregnant female. Later, I learned these lemurs need to eat a large amount of the tough stems in order to get the nutrients from the bamboo. This makes their bellies protrude. As yet, scientists do not know how these lemurs detoxify after eating their favorite food.

Bamboo lemurs are also called gentle lemurs, perhaps explaining why this particular lemur didn't mind my staring at him. I marveled at nature's brilliance. *Is that specialization or what?* I thought. *There is so much to study on this amazing island.*

Night Adventure with a Brown Mouse Lemur

Mark invited us to join him on a night adventure. There was a good chance to see the rare Brown Mouse Lemur, the smallest lemur and the smallest primate in the world. An adult can weigh up to 3.4 ounces with a body length of less than five inches, and a thick tail of the same length. His agile tail helps balance him as he navigates the branches in his domain and the tail will store fat as needed. If the brown mouse lemur is able to evade natural predators such as the cat-like fossa, mongoose, hawks, and owls, he can live up to eight years in a tropical rainforest.

This lemur sounded so cute, I really wanted to see one. Tiny animals fascinate me, so I was willing to trek another steep and slippery hillside at dusk to reach the shelter where naturalists and park rangers observe the brown mouse lemurs. Park rangers have been putting out pieces of ripe bananas for years where these nocturnal animals show up to feast most evenings.

Mark warned us that nothing was certain, but we kept our fingers crossed and we waited patiently in an opening carved out of the thick dripping rainforest. Some people in our group escaped the drizzle by sitting under a picnic shelter complete with table and benches, similar to the one where we had eaten lunch earlier in the day. There were eight in our group, plus a few other visitors and several guides. One of the guides picked a ripe banana out of his box and smeared the smashed pulp onto a nearby branch. Then he cut another banana in half and impaled it on a pointed stick next to the trail.

We talked in hushed tones among ourselves, all lights off, anticipating the main event. A sharp-eyed guide suddenly whispered, "Here he comes."

A chipmunk-sized lemur with thick gray-brown fur, his ears twitching, crept out of the bushes for his nightly gorge on the smashed banana. For a few moments, he looked at us with huge eyes and sniffed the fragrant offering. His long tail hung limp as he licked the banana pulp. Our flashing cameras did not bother him at all.

Another guide pointed behind him where a second mouse lemur sat on his haunches next to the speared banana. His tiny paws propped on the peel's cut edge, he nibbled leisurely on the sweet pulp and watched us as he chewed. I wondered, *Why don't the flashes bother his night-sensitive eyes the same as most owls? He doesn't even flinch at all as they go off.*

Someone behind me observed, "That little mouse is worth millions to the country's economy." I hated that comment, possibly true, but it spoiled the moment for me.

The mouse lemur's big eyes swept across our adoring faces as if acknowledging his own popularity. Suddenly he turned, flicked his tail, and sprang three feet up on to a branch and disappeared into the bushes. I was in awe of the incredible distance he covered effortlessly! Once again, it was another memorable moment in Madagascar.

On the Road Again

After two nights and days in the park cherishing the memories of the lemurs in Ranomafana, we returned to the main road to continue north toward our next birding site, stopping along the way for birds, as usual. The long day of driving included a visit to a country market and our only cultural experience, both rich with impressions and delights.

In the highlands, every available piece of land is terraced, primarily for rice cultivation. Here and there, small plots of vegetables and eucalyptus forests for timber crawled up the hillsides. Tile roofs topped the two- and three-story houses made from the mud bricks we saw being made earlier. Because of the mild weather and fertile soil, this is where most of the Malagasy live, and an even higher percentage of the Merina who were the first settlers in Madagascar.

We were on our way to our last adventure of the tour, this time driving north to Perinet Reserve, 85 miles east of Antananarivo in central Madagascar.

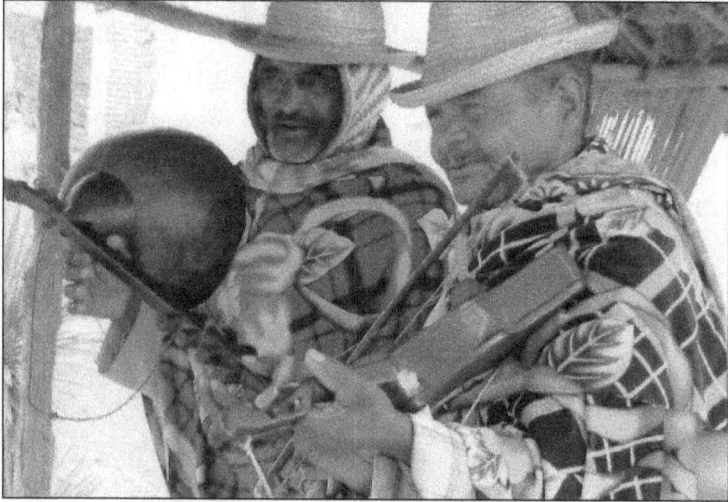

Musicians in Antanifotsy, central Madagascar

CHAPTER 8

A Country Market and a Bit of Culture

On our way to Perinet Reserve, we stopped to visit a local market and experience some local culture. Of course, we searched for birds in the fields, towns, and cities along the way. In spite of the denser population in the highlands of Madagascar, birds congregate in marshes, ponds, and fields close to towns.

About 100 miles north of Ranomafana, we stopped for a birding break just outside of Antanifotsy, the eighth largest city in Madagascar. The pleasantly cool weather felt lovely after the hot and humid tropical jungle at Ranomafana.

My Search for a Lamba

Our guide Rivo and I were chatting while we waited by the bus for the others to return after scanning a small marshy area for birds. Farmers were working in some terraced fields above the marsh and I spotted a curious teenager wrapped in one of the bright lambas.

I poked my chin toward the boy's lamba and said, "Rivo, I want one of those, where can I buy one?" reminding him of my previous request.

"You don't want one of them," said Rivo. "They are just a style, not traditional at all."

"But I like it. I want one," I insisted.

"Oh, no. Those people used to wear blankets here when it got cold. Then they started wearing towels. Yellow towels! "He paused so that would sink in and I'd get the point of how ridiculous I might look in a lamba. "Now, they like those colored lambas."

"I want one."

"Well, you can't even wear it in Tana," Rivo scoffed, as if that would matter to me.

He sounded a bit condescending and that's when I remembered that he was probably a Merina, the tribe that occupied a privileged position in Madagascar. He had access to resources unavailable to the farmers we were watching. Rivo had a good sense of humor, so when he tried to discourage me, I wanted a lamba even more, and I wanted to wear it in Tana where Rivo could see.

The first time I saw one of the garish lambas, an ox cart driver on a dusty coastal road had wrapped it around his head and shoulders, which certainly set him apart from his companions, who wore more neutral clothing. In the highlands, even more people were wearing the bright wraps festooned with huge red, blue, and orange flowers on a red background. The colorful lambas were popular in this cooler climate because the fabric is an inexpensive, lightweight velvet that is heavier and warmer than lambas from other regions of Madagascar. I knew fashions changed and if these garish lambas had replaced the yellow towels, who knows what they were wearing more than fifteen years later?

I was in luck. Mark had planned a visit to a weekly Saturday market close by, set up behind the playing field of a large school. *Maybe I can find a lamba there,* I thought.

When we arrived at 11:00, the market activities were well under way. Items for purchase or trade overflowed the stalls or lay in neat piles on tarps on the ground. Customers examined the wares of hardware vendors, miscellaneous metal, bolts, pieces of motors, and other machine parts. Nearby, a man had lined up new bicycles for inspection. Used bikes stood in another row. One vendor stood next to wheels, spokes, gears, and chains. All the scrap metal lay near to the car park and the vendors were mostly women. The gleaned metal included pipes, railings, wire, and bits of appliances.

The vendors hunched behind their displays, chatted among themselves, and watched for customers. People strolled the aisles and after fingering the goods, they made a few purchases but that did not really seem to be the focus of the gathering. This country market provided the opportunity for a social gathering and a little time to relax after a hard week of work.

I like to see what is for sale in hardware stores when I travel, alert for things people actually use in their daily lives. For instance, every time I lightly touch the cane wrapping around the shiny, brittle, heat-conserving core of a Chinese thermos bottle, I remember the trip I took with my mother to China. Though I don't use the thermos, I still have it because the fond memories rekindle my delight in the trip.

In that Madagascar market, I lingered next to a vendor wearing a suit jacket and straw hat, busily cranking the fan for a tiny forge to heat his soldering iron. I'd seen this basic set up in Mexico. The iron is a square lump of heavy metal pointed at one end with a handle. The vendor heated it on a flame and soldered until the iron lost its heat. The man's customer, also wearing a well-worn suit jacket and a fedora, watched the process with the same fascination as I did. The repairman patched a hole in an enamel bowl. I wondered if the men knew that solder contains lead and the bowl would be poisonous if they used it for food. In a poor economy where nothing goes to waste, I knew the bowl had many other uses, so I hoped they would be safe.

Up the hill, a pig squealed when the seller pinned the unhappy animal to the ground while the potential buyer pulled out the pig's tongue for inspection. In the same area, a cheerful young fellow climbed on his bike and pedaled off with a squirming piglet under one arm. Vendors displayed small piles of charcoal next to the half-full charcoal bags similar to the ones we saw lining the road from the coast. Drivers had parked their decorative zebu carts next to brightly colored strands of nylon rope. I wondered why I didn't see any sisal ropes since farmers grow sisal in the south for its fiber. There were a few woven sisal baskets for sale, but not many. I had seen a few sisal baskets where tourists visited, but this market was not for tourists. Later, I learned that sisal from Madagascar is an important export because of its high quality. Most commercial sisal is grown on plantations, not on small farms, so perhaps local farmers grew this market's sisal for local use by the women who made the baskets.

Further up the slope, vendors clustered their rows of temporary stalls according to product areas. Attractive displays of local vegetables, including potatoes, carrots, beans, peas, cauliflower, tomatoes, lettuce, and cucumbers drew potential customers in to test their freshness. Vendors piled beans and rice into mounds in the mouths of cloth bags, topped by enamel measuring pans. Nearby they displayed yellow, brown, and black spices in sealed plastic bags. Artful displays of beads, jewelry, makeup, bowls, candles, shoes, combs—just about anything a department store or grocery store might have—flowed into the aisles.

Off to the side, I watched a hopeful young man hover near a teenage girl selling hot beans and rice. A short distance away, two wizened women guffawed at something known only to them, a private joke or a rude comment. The market brimmed with life and all of its senses. I was exhilarated and grateful to be a part of this thriving marketplace in a land I had dreamt about for many years.

Suddenly, something red caught my eye. I quickened my step, briskly moving past the children's clothes waving gently in the breeze and past the customers picking over heaps of used T-shirts. At last, I found lengths of the lamba cloth displayed, one or two to a vendor, among sedate fabric for dresses and skirts. I asked one vendor his price, and then some others. Each time I asked, the price went up, so I returned to the first vendor and bought one of his lambas. It was made of stretchy synthetic cloth, fuzzy on one side with a blood red background and the garish red, blue, and yellow flowers. This was so unlike what I normally buy, which usually consisted of natural fabrics and muted colors.

Back at the bus, I wrapped my new lamba around me, jauntily tossing one end over my shoulder, and modeled my find for Rivo. I loved my lamba. My friends snapped my photo, Rivo smiled, and then he quietly stepped back to disassociate himself from my display. This made my smile even bigger.

Food, Music & Dance

After our visit to the market, we drove into Antanifotsy, a city of 70,000 people, for our lunch and some unusual and delightful entertainment. A bamboo fence surrounded a small outdoor stage for an entertainment venue, built in a rather steep bowl. We sat at two picnic tables sheltered by grass roofs on the only flat spot in the venue.

When we arrived the food was ready for us. Servers brought heaping bowls of rice and smaller bowls of a tasty beef stew, along with lovely vegetables on the side. This was the only meal during our trip that might approximate what the local Malagasy eat since we ate at places that catered to tourists.

As I ate, I mused about the food we had been served during the trip. Rice is the staple of the Malagasy diet, brought from Borneo by the first settlers. I doubt we did justice to the heaps of white rice served everywhere in Madagascar. A typical Malagasy eats a kilo (2.2 lbs.) of rice per day—a big heap of rice with every meal— and small portions of meat and vegetables as a side to the rice. As tourists, we did the opposite, eating big portions of meat or seafood and a small helping of rice.

In the coastal area of Ifaty, we had eaten delicious seafood, including everything from the charred, whole, snapper-like fish to shrimp, prawns, and mangrove crabs. In the rainforest at Ranomafana, we saw sleek zebus, well fed on the fast growing tropical plants. I suspected the rainforest zebus were a meat source for our meals in other parts of the country where the zebus were too scrawny to be served to *vazaha* like us. The occasional bits of free-range chicken and even some pork, were always tough but flavorful. We ate a good variety of the highland-grown vegetables that were usually found in local markets.

For desserts, we had every restaurant's version of bananas flambé and even a pineapple flambé. Occasionally, the dessert choices included fresh tropical fruit, crepes, or flan. I am not familiar enough with French cuisine to know how much it influenced the food we ate, but the French-trained staff took a long time to prepare the food and serve it. Throughout our travels, our guides did their best to hasten the service because after an early breakfast, followed by a long day of birding, we needed a quick dinner and then off to bed. Most nights there wasn't time for a leisurely meal.

We always drank bottled water and a few people drank tea with meals, while many more drank coffee at breakfast. The Malagasy also drink tea and coffee, but their favorite drink is *ranonapongo,* also called *ranovola,* or burnt rice water. They pour boiled water in the rice-encrusted pan used for cooking rice for the meal and let it cool a bit. It's an acquired taste, they say, and I never saw it on any of our menus. I doubt the places where we ate would have had *ranovola* available even if we had asked to try it.

The Local Entertainment

At our quaint restaurant in Antanifotsy, we finished our simple meal and waited for the next phase of our cultural experience. While the singers prepared the stage, we had time to use the bathroom facilities, such as they were. While on the road, we sometimes used Asian-style outhouses, which are basically holes in the floor of a tiny, often airy, outhouse. This situation was similar, maybe worse. The outhouse was uphill from the picnic tables, which caused me to wonder about the drainage—a rude question guests should not ask the host. Two other women from our group waited at the outhouse door when I approached. A voice from inside said, "I don't know about this. It feels rather risky." The other two laughed, but did not leave. When my turn came, I discovered why it seemed risky. The wooden floor felt quite spongy, sagging noticeably when I placed my feet beside the open slot in the middle of the floor. I weighed my need against the possibility of plunging into the dark below. I unbuckled my pants and thought, *Travel has its risks.*

Once we all regrouped at the picnic tables, the entertainment began. Two lively older men with stubbly beards and big smiles stepped to the front of the small stage. Both men wore garish, red, sarong-like lambdas, a lot like mine, draped around their shoulders. The bright lambdas framed their dark leathered faces, topped by small straw hats. A round-faced man put his simple homemade violin to his shoulder, while his friend adjusted on his right shoulder a banjo-like instrument that had a large gourd for its sound box. To play this fascinating instrument, he plucked the two strings with his right hand, and changed between two notes with his left hand by pressing the strings against pegs that protruded from the instrument's neck.

The toothless men gummed the words to lively local songs, delighting each other with their apparent improvisation. They sang with gusto and raced to the finish, laughing as they lowered their instruments to our applause. Their uninhibited performance inspired good tips from our grateful audience. Rivo told us later that the songs they sang were adapted from ones that would have lasted much longer had they been part of a traditional ceremony to communicate with the ancestors.

The dancers were small women who wore light green cotton skirts, white blouses, and straw hats. When the dancers invited us to partner with them, the last woman in the dance troupe grabbed me. She lined us up for a couple of circuits around the stage, which was basically a shuffling step to the beat of the music. I smiled graciously, but was grateful when we stopped. As soon as my dance partner allowed me to escape, I hurried back to my table. That group participation felt just too contrived for my taste and seemed to be a cultural stretch in order to please the tourists, many of whom I'm sure loved it. I'm an introvert and am always a reluctant participant in these touristy events.

However, I appreciated the presentation for its small slice of Malagasy culture and local flavor. There was lots of potential for tourism to grow and increase local economic development, and I was glad to be a part of this local tourist venue.

Female Red-bellied Lemur and her babies, Perinet National Park

CHAPTER 9

Birds, Kids, and Lemurs at Perinet Reserve

We arrived at Perinet Reserve after a long but interesting drive from Ranomafana National Park. Located three hours east of Antananarivo in central Madagascar, Perinet Reserve is one of the easiest rainforest parks to reach from the capital. This reserve is now a national park called Andasibe-Mantaida National Park to acknowledge that the original, much larger forest, has been divided in two by heavy logging and destructive cyclones that blow in from the Indian Ocean.

A healthy population of the endangered Indri Indri Lemur, the largest lemurs, thrives at the Perinet Preserve. The double name indicates that this species is the one by which all other indri lemurs are compared for purposes of identification.

Efforts to reintroduce two other threatened lemurs, the Diademed Safika and Black-and-white Lemurs, back into their historical habitat have been quite successful. However, continued logging of the rain-forest adjacent to the park and replanting with more marketable eucalyptus and pine trees, have ruined chances for enlarging the lemurs' habitat. We hoped to see all three types of lemurs during our three days at the preserve.

Another Fabulous Birding Moment

On our first morning at Perinet, we had good luck spotting birds along a dirt road near a brushy creek in the park. The drizzle had tapered off and the sun peeked through the clouds when our park guide, Alex, stopped. "Listen," he whispered as he cupped his hands around his ears to pin down the direction of the call. I hadn't heard a thing, but as usual, our guide knew what birds might be in the area. Finding a particular bird depends on many things, but I know guides are relieved to hear the call of a difficult bird.

Then I heard a soft "boop" from deep in the forest.

"That's it," Alex softly confirmed. The timid sound came again. "Boop."

"It's a Short-legged Ground-roller." Alex's eyes sparkled, always a good sign that the bird is special. He beckoned us to follow. Only three of us slipped off the road and into the brush. The others waited for us to return, not wanting to risk wet shoes in the marshy ground after a rainy morning full of great birds.

We four birders thrashed through the thick under-brush, attempting to be quiet as we pulled off vines that grabbed our clothing. We ducked under fallen branches and crossed a stream on an impromptu log bridge. Suddenly, Alex held up his flat hand, the signal for us to stop, and pointed up into a tree. About fifteen feet above us, a pudgy bird the size of a child's football, sat on a small branch. We easily saw the short-legged ground-roller with his bronze-green back and his brown and white belly. Then his mouth opened, his body quivered, and we heard the call, a soprano "boop."

The bird continued calling, slow and questioning. At every call, his squat body did a little shimmy. He seemed undisturbed by the commotion at the foot of the tree where we stared up at him. We hardly needed binoculars but we carefully raised them to drink in each shaking feather, each placid eye. There is nothing better than actually seeing a bird make a call, which cements that sound to memory.

While we watched, a drab-colored female flew in and landed in a nearby bush. A bright red, eight-inch millipede squirmed in her thick bill—something for the babies. She looked at us for a moment and then flew up the hill. Her mate continued his hooting.

I savored every detail of such a sweet bird in this incredible rainforest environment, unique only to Madagascar. My love for this hot and humid island country, rich with animals and plant life, filled me with joy and gratitude. I noted to myself, *Another fabulous moment.*

Children Sing About the Kestrel

Birds wisely rest during the oppressive afternoons in tropical climates, so we had the choice of several activities our first day in Perinet. One group chose to visit a school and then go shopping. When I later heard about their encounter with the kids, I was sorry I hadn't gone with them. Rivo had asked some school children to sing the song about the kestrel that he had tried to teach us on the bus. The children joined hands and circled each other, singing gaily about the Madagascar kestrel.

Fellow traveler Don captured it all on his small video camera. Then, Don gathered the kids around him and played it back. The unfamiliar images surprised the children and they exploded into screams of delight before they could even hear their own voices coming from the recording. They ran around jumping high into the air, hugging each other, clapping, and laughing. After Don told me the story, I wondered, *How would the kids have reacted if they had heard us struggling to learn the song they sang?* Since our bus driver thought our singing attempts were hysterical, I'm sure the kids would've reacted with something far more exuberant than the screaming and jumping!

Harassment or Passion?

In the spiny forest in southwestern Madagascar the guides gently herded birds across the path where we waited to see them. They did not seem stressed with our presence, perhaps because only a limited number of birders visit that area. However, many more visitors visit the eastern rainforests like Perinet, which is so close to Tana and so easily accessible. The eastern rainforests are popular places where up to four groups a day may try and see the same bird. Local Malagasy guides use taped birdcalls to draw territorial birds into the open, but after too many taped calls from the same "bird" the real birds seem to know there is no threat and don't respond. These practices frustrate serious birders and their guides as well. I was about to experience this frustration firsthand.

On the afternoon in Perinet dedicated to the school visit and shopping, I chose the alternative, the pursuit of another marsh bird. Again, David and I were the only ones eager enough to join Alex on that baking hot afternoon. Alex assured David and me that he could attract a particularly rare bird with a taped birdcall. "Oh, no problem. The bird will come right to our feet."

I had never experienced using a taped call to attract a particular bird and could not have anticipated the problem I had with the encounter. On that baking-hot afternoon jaunt, David and I expected to observe a Gray Emutail, which is a small marsh warbler. My passion for pretty birds was unquestionable, so after lunch I checked my bird book and found a drawing of an unremarkable bird, the grey emutail. Even though my enthusiasm for the afternoon's trip was tepid, we had not seen that bird and I told myself at least it was better than shopping.

We took a short bus trip down the road and pulled over. We followed our guide along an irrigation ditch, across a rice paddy dike, and on through cultivated fields for half an hour. Alex stopped at an earthen dam that held back a pond almost filled in by reeds and marsh grasses. We listened for a call, facing the marsh. Then Alex turned on his tape player and we heard the recorded call of the gray emutail, a rattling *chuchuchuchuk*.

Nothing. No answering call.

We tried another spot, still no results. Finally, we teetered along the side of a very steep bank. Alex stopped next to a ten-foot-wide swath of open water that separated us from the reeds. He seemed to be getting nervous.

"I was here two years ago and this is where the birds were," Alex explained. "They came right to my feet, truly."

He played the tape again. This time we heard a distant reply. Then, out of the corner of my eye I caught the rustle of reeds and a brown flash just as Alex pointed. "There," he gasped, but by the time he raised his arm he was pointing at empty air.

I recalled marsh wrens at home that skulk among reeds, but when their territory is threatened they will pop up and hang on the reed top and call out their challenge. However, even with persistent use of the taped call that day this emutail refused to show himself again.

"This water was not here," Alex noted. "The local people have cleared this place recently and now the birds do not come."

Alex rewound and played his tape repeatedly. I began to feel uncomfortable for the little bird. "OK, I'm happy," I said. "I saw it, kind of, and heard the call. Let's go back."

"Oh, just up here, maybe he will come just ahead," Alex responded hopefully with a hint of worry. He headed up the slope another ten feet. Once again, he played the tape with no results.

"Let's stop now," I insisted, irritated with Alex's persistence that looked like harassment at that point. I thought, *How much clearer can I be?* I turned to go and he followed, looking back one more time.

My Birding Approach

Some birders are called "listers" because they keep a list of every bird they see and take pride in the number. A hardcore lister would not have given up as I did without a good look at the bird, but that trip was early in my birding career. I do keep track of the birds I see, but after a reasonable try, I am happy with a glimpse or a song that I note in my records, especially if it is a rare bird to see or hear. At the very least, I am happy just to know I was in the *presence* of the bird in his environment.

Birders know that hearing a distinct call "counts" in the birding community. The story passed around is that a birding group initiated this convention after trying to flush a different rare marsh bird by shuffling through its habitat in an attempt to scare it out of hiding. On their next pass over the same spot, they discovered that someone had stepped on the poor thing. This may be a myth, but the point is valid. Birding protocol must include leaving the bird as comfortable as before we arriving—or at least alive!

Lemur Families

On the second day, we drove to the Mantiada portion of the park connected to the Andasibe portion only by a corridor. This is where it is sometimes possible to see the troops of indri lemurs. Researchers have been studying the lemurs in this park for years, and while the lemurs there are not tame, they are accustomed to people and go about their daily routines undisturbed. We had high hopes of observing lemur families in Andasibe-Mantiada National Park.

We followed a trail into the thick humid forest and kept our eyes glued to the trees for unusual shaking and our ears pricked for animal noises. Suddenly, I noticed movement in the canopy of some distant tamarind trees and a quick flash of a lemur's body. We halted, hoping the lemurs might come in our direction. We were thrilled to see that they were indeed approaching. I could see long arms and legs spread to catch the limbs of the next tree and light colored bodies running up long branches to gain height and then leap with confidence.

Mark gasped, then with a tone of reverence and awe exclaimed, "I've never seen these lemurs in all the times I've visited Madagascar; these are Black-and-White Ruffed Lemurs." Since I had never seen any lemurs before this trip, every one was awesome but I had to recognize that this sighting was even more special.

A black-and-white ruffed lemur is a medium-sized lemur that weighs up to 9 pounds, and is up to 21 inches tall from head to length of their torso. These lemurs are highly endangered largely due to the degradation of their habitat by loggers and farmers.

We followed the lemurs' raucous vocalizations as they raced through the trees. At one point, they paused right above us and we could see that their black tails were longer than their black-and-white bodies. I loved the white fluffy ruffs around their black necks and ears that accentuated their bright brown eyes. They easily outdistanced us and soon we lost them—but not the thrill of the brief encounter. For me, that experience with the lemurs will last a lifetime.

An hour later, Mark stopped us. He pointed up into the branches of a tree close to the trail. "There they are, indri indri," he whispered.

A family of indri lemurs, or babakoto in Malagasy, rested in the crotches of several trees close to our trail. These tree dwellers are the largest lemurs in Madagascar and can weigh up to 20 pounds and grow up to 27 inches in length. The indri is the only lemur with a short vestigial tail of 2 inches. The lemur closest to us was black and white, but had a different pattern from the previous family. At first, we could only see a distortion of the belly fur, but soon I made out a baby's tiny arm that reached around to her mother's back and firmly gripped her fur.

The female had a fuzzy body, round ears, and bright yellow eyes, and she lay on her back on a sturdy branch that served as her lounge chair, gripping the tree trunk for stability. The mother turned her triangular black face in our direction and blinked. She seemed uninterested in us and unbothered by our intrusion.

Other family members around this mother lemur began feeding again. An older sibling ambled to the end of a nearby branch, delicately pulled a flower to his mouth, and nibbled the petals. The baby awakened and squirmed. When the little one spotted us, we could see his head and his large curious eyes. The baby crawled up his mother's belly and turned sideways, belly-to-belly with Mom. At first, he looked like he might slide off her slippery fur and drop, but he held on and squirmed to drape his little bottom clear of her side. Then he let loose a tiny golden stream, urinating into the branches. When done, the infant climbed back onto her chest and began some practice leaps to the next vertical limb no more than two feet away. He leapt and then looked back at Mom, who was watching. Dare I say she looked on proudly? He leapt back to the safety of her lap, then took another leap away and returned, gaining confidence as he explored the world beyond his mother's embrace.

While observing the baby lemur, we heard a distant eerie call that reminded me of a humpback whale's song. The mother lemur heard it as well. She sat up, lifted her head, and formed her mouth in a wide "O," revealing the ruby red inside her cheeks. She tensed and with a piercing wail, let out a lemur call that slid down an octave, paused in her lower vocal range, and then lifted at the end. This firm reply claimed her territory.

After calling for several minutes, the female shinnied up the trunk of the tree, her infant glued to her back. She paused briefly, sprang in a high arc and grabbed the next tree. She clutched the trunk with her strong legs and then bounced confidently from tree to tree with the speed of a rubber ball.

After the sound of their leaving faded, Mark said, "All species of indri are quite vocal, communicating with singing, roaring, and other creative vocalizations."

Oh, how I wish I could have hung around there to witness those sweet family activities and to hear more of those creative vocalizations. Once again, Madagascar's unique beauty filled me with delight and reverence. Our tour would soon be over, so I paused for another moment to drink it all in.

White-browed Owl (Madagascar Hawk-Owl),
photographed through a telescope.

CHAPTER 10

Farewell to Madagascar

On our last morning, I awoke with a sense of sadness and disappointment that our wildlife tour in Madagascar was coming to an end. My traveling companions felt the same. We had a few precious hours to enjoy this unique and environmentally rich country, so I jumped at the opportunity to see one last endemic bird in the Perinet rainforest. After that, we had a three-hour drive to Tana, and a long plane ride home.

The Search for One More Bird

Rivo learned from another guide that a Madagascar Flufftail had been seen a short drive from our lodge. It was a long shot, but Rivo told us, "The flufftail will defend its territory even out of breeding season, and I am optimistic that it will be calling."

That was enough for me—I was ready to go! A light rain was falling when we reached the site. Most of the tired birders stayed in the dry van, but I popped up my umbrella and joined six diehards who followed Rivo into the wet forest. My soggy shoes squeaked as I walked along the muddy trail, but I was warmer than I would have been at home in Oregon in late October.

At a sharp bend in the trail, Rivo signaled us to stop and settle ourselves. We quietly folded our umbrellas, strange objects that could scare local birds. Fat raindrops rolled off the rainforest canopy, quickly soaking us. Rivo hooted, imitating the flufftail call, challenging the bird to defend its territory. After several tries, I heard a soft sound from far back in the forest. *Was that the bird?* I wondered, but Rivo did not seem excited.

Rivo hooted again. We peered into the lush underbrush hoping for any telltale movement. Glossy leaves shuddered and flicked off the falling drops. *Was that quivering leaf a bird, or just another drop off a leaf?*

Several times I thought with eager anticipation, *Maybe that's the flufftail,* but disappointment followed a few seconds later.

One of my fellow birders picked a leech off her neck. For ten long minutes, we waited for another hoot that did not come. Rivo shrugged his shoulders and we turned back for the bus. We did not see the bird.

On the trail back to the bus, my feet squishing in my soggy shoes, feeling a bit chilled in spite of the humidity, I asked myself, *What am I doing here?*

Then I remembered the delightful lemurs, stunning birds, forests teeming with new creatures, and the interesting people we had seen and enjoyed in a place none of us had known before our three weeks in Madagascar. *This* is what I want to remember, the wonderland of the cute, the exotic, the silly, as well as the less delightful creatures that added interest to our trip.

Madagascar's Environmental Decline

I had been prescient when I worried about the country's environmental concerns before taking the trip to Madagascar, and, the degradation of this unique country that has resumed since then. After our trip in 2004 and until 2009, President Marc Ravalomanana designated several areas we had visited as national parks and wildlife reserves. This news greatly buoyed my spirits but the momentum did not last.

In 2009, Andry Rajoelina, the opposition leader, led a violent coup to become the president of Madagascar. He rescinded protection of the environmental preserves, after which, international conservation groups cut off all funding. The park management collapsed. With the country in chaos, 82 percent of the people sank into extreme poverty. Desperate, people killed wildlife for food and poached trees for export.

By 2015, eleven years after our visit, the population had increased from 18 million to 23 million due to local customs and weak reproductive health care. This growing population exacted a terrible toll on the already eroded and parched land. Madagascar's first legitimate president, Hery Rajaonarimampianina, was elected in 2015 and has done nothing to change the destructive policies of his predecessor. Redemption was possible when we visited, but only with strong, well-funded, and organized efforts. As of 2018, the future looks grim for Madagascar's environment and wildlife.

Reflections

I don't regret visiting Madagascar in spite of its current problems. I remember the idyllic forests filled with a rich variety of wildlife, delightful to see and filled with promise for new discoveries. In contrast, memories of the enormous swaths of sterile red clay still haunt me. There is little hope of recovery for the land that supports such an important collection of plants and animals.

So, what good did our visit do for the promotion of tourism if there is nothing left for visitors to see? And what good did it do now that we must cut back on travel to save the planet? My heart aches both for the people of Madagascar who can no longer depend on the land for a sustainable lifestyle and for the natural resources that will soon be gone because of the people's increasing desperation. Often, I have thought about what will happen among the people who live in Madagascar. Will they become violent or hopeless? I ask myself, *Is this what we all could face if changes are not made soon to save the global environment?*

And what of the possible medical discoveries predicted by scientists, like the recent use of the rosy periwinkle known for its anti-cancer properties, especially for leukemia and other blood cancers? I must count on a miracle.

This is a sorry conclusion for my remarkable trip to Madagascar, but I continue with my fight for a green planet. I minimize my environmental impact by living a simple life and making financial gifts to organizations that fight for a healthy planet. Even though I will not be around to see the outcome, I hope future generations will see the amazing creatures of Madagascar, just as I did. Now, more than ever, I realize how fortunate I have been to see this land firsthand.

Bhutan
SOUTHEAST
ASIA

2004

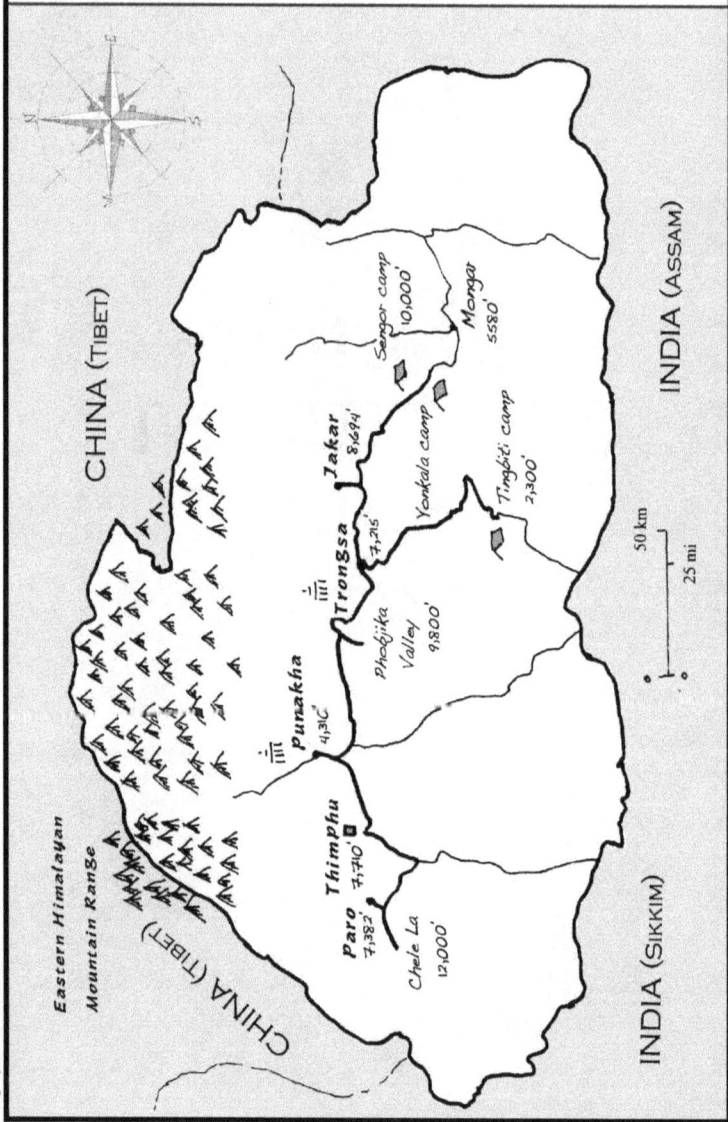

Routes and Campsites in
BHUTAN

CHINA (TIBET)

INDIA (ASSAM)

CHINA (TIBET)

INDIA (SIKKIM)

Eastern Himalayan
Mountain Range

Sengor camp
10,000'

Mongar
5580'

Jakar
8,694'

Yonkala camp

Trongsa
7,215'

Tingbri camp
2,300'

Punakha
4,130'

Phobjika
Valley
9,800'

Thimphu
7,710'

Paro
7,382'

Chele La
12,000'

50 km

25 mi

Map by Harriet Denison

Introduction

Bhutan is one of those mysterious countries I first encountered as a youngster reading National Geographic. The people's colorful clothing and their old ornate architecture featured in the magazine's photos opened my eyes to another fascinating culture in a far off place in the world. As an adult, occasional news items mentioned Bhutan, in particular its precarious political situation and its concept of the Gross National Happiness Index to measure progress. I also knew that for years the country did not welcome tourists, so I had put a possible visit on the backburner of my world travels.

I began birding internationally in 2001 and had taken trips to far away places such as Antarctica and Madagascar. A long list of countries still called to me, and at the age of 64, I felt pressure to do the difficult tours soon, before I aged out of the more challenging physical demands. In 2007, Field Guides offered a three-week birding tour in Bhutan. I jumped at the opportunity to take this tour with a popular birding company known for its excellent guides.

Located in Southeast Asia, Bhutan lies southeast of Nepal, a larger and better-known neighbor. Both countries are squeezed between the geographical giants of India to the south, and to the north the controversial Tibetan Autonomous Region controlled by China.

The landscape of Bhutan stretches from the subtropical plains that border India to the subalpine heights in the north with fingers of land stretching into the southern Himalayas and mountain passes over 12,000 feet. Bhutan's extremes in geography and climate create a wide range of biodiversity and ecosystems, which provide rich opportunities for observing a great number of the 670 recorded bird species.

A Brief History of Bhutan

The early history of the land now known as Bhutan is uncertain and shrouded in mythology. However, this territory situated along the ancient trade route through Eurasia, known as the Silk Road, maintained its independence while so many places were colonized by the more powerful nations. In the 7th century, a Tibetan ruler ordered the construction of several Buddhist temples in Bhutan, eventually establishing Bhutan as a Buddhist Theocracy with numerous fiefdoms. For centuries after that introduction of Buddhism, wars and civil unrest caused political borders to shift among the small Bhutanese monarchies tucked into the river valleys.

In the late 1800s, Ugyen Wangchuck (b. 1862) the governor of the district of Trongsa in central Bhutan, consolidated power by uniting the smaller monarchies. In 1907, after ruling unofficially for decades, governors of the districts in Bhutan chose Ugyen Wangchuck as the First Hereditary King of Bhutan. He reigned until his death in 1926.

For years, British India had engaged in trade treaties with the various monarchs so First King Ugyen Wangchuck continued to build those ties. Britain agreed to advise but not to interfere with the new monarchy, a demand that has served Bhutan well. First King Wangchuck maintained only weak ties with British India.

Second King Jigme Wangchuck, the son of First King Wangchuck, reigned from 1926 to 1952 and continued his father's work. Bhutan was largely unaffected by the Great Depression in the United States and World War II because of its isolation. When Britain pulled out of India in 1947, all political ties with Bhutan officially ended. However, Bhutan continued to welcome India and Britain's advice on international matters. At the time, Bhutan lost some lowland areas to Britain but in return it received an annual stipend from Britain, and later, from India.

Third King Jigme Dorji Wangchuck, who reigned from 1952 to 1972, began the country's modernization in response to the Chinese annexation of Tibet in 1959. As part of a plan to increase international ties, Bhutan allowed a few closely monitored tourists to enter the country. The king believed that Bhutan would be better recognized as a nation if it became a democracy like Britain. Third King Wangchuck began the long process toward democratization by establishing criteria for citizenship in the Kingdom of Bhutan in order to deal with increasing immigration. To be a citizen, the applicant had to have either a Bhutanese father or proof of ten years residence in Bhutan. King Wangchuck also banned further immigration of Nepalese, who were the bulk of the new immigrants.

During the next twenty years, Third King Wangchuck moved Bhutan out of isolation and into global participation as a democratic nation. He established a National Assembly (the first unicameral Parliament), developed a Bhutanese Army, laid the groundwork for an educational system throughout Bhutan, joined the Universal Postal Union, and in 1971 established Bhutan as a member of the United Nations. Third King Wangchuck officially ended feudalism, redistributed land to the poor, and built roads and infrastructure in the country.

Third King Wangchuck wanted his people to have good governance and a sustainable, equitable economy. He wanted to preserve the treasured ecology of the country and the cultural vitality while at the same time moving toward modern democracy. For all his efforts to bring Bhutan into the 20th century, he became known as the "Father of Modern Bhutan."

After the sudden death of Third King Wangchuck in 1972, his successor, Fourth King Jigme Singye Wangchuck, reigned from 1972 to 2006. He further accelerated the modernization of Bhutan by focusing on self-sufficiency and expanding the country's income. By the early 1980s, cautious Bhutan became more welcoming to visitors by establishing a national airline officially named Royal Bhutan Airlines. Bhutan's Airlines is commonly called Druk Air in a nod to the king who is called the Druk Gyalpo, which means the "Dragon King of Bhutan" in Dzongkha, the national language.

In 1974, Fourth King Wangchuck, made an offhanded remark to his advisers about promoting gross national happiness instead of the gross national product used by other countries to measure development. He outlined four important goals that he derived from his father's work: good governance, sustainable socio-economic development, preservation, and promotion of culture and environmental conservatism. These goals are now enshrined in Bhutan's constitution passed by the National Assembly in 2008 and established as an essential part of Bhutan's new democracy. The tool for measuring that dream is now known as the Gross National Happiness Index and the country's measurement for successful development. This is a remarkable concept that continues to evolve as more countries work to incorporate the idea of a Gross National Happiness Index.

Bhutan's Ethnic Groups

Bhutan has three primary ethnic groups. The Ngalop and Sharchop people practice Buddhism and speak Dzongkha. Together, these two groups are known as Drukpas. The third primary group is the Lhotshampa who practice Hinduism and speak Nepali. Before Bhutan's first official census in 1988, demographic estimates varied widely.

The most powerful of the ethnic groups are the Ngalops who first came to Bhutan from Tibet in the 9th century and now inhabit the northern and western part of the country. The Sharchops are a mix of Tibetan and other ethnicities from adjacent countries and they now inhabit the southeastern part of Bhutan. The Lhotshampas, which means "southerners," began migrating to southern Bhutan in the late 19th century. Government policies discouraged their movement into the higher positions of Bhutan although some Lhotshampas hold government positions. As the numbers of Lhotshampas grew, the government claimed that many of them were illegal immigrants. Changes in Bhutan's immigration policies lead to violent protests among the Lhotshampas who demanded their place in the country's emerging democracy. The Bhutanese government responded by forcing out more than 100,000 Lhotshampas from the country. I would learn about all of this in much greater detail after my trip to Bhutan in 2007, and I discuss Bhutan's ethnic rivalries in further detail.

Good Timing for a Visit

By a stroke of luck, we toured Bhutan on the cusp of a new king's coronation. Fifth King Jigme Khesar Namgyel Wangchuck became Bhutan's first constitutional monarch in 2008, the year after our tour. Two years prior to the coronation, his father, Fourth King Wangchuck, abdicated the throne to emphasize the transition of the country to a democracy, diminishing the power of the monarchy by design. He arranged for the new king's formal ascension to the throne to be on November 6, 2008 at 8:31 a.m., deemed the most auspicious moment to assure a successful reign.

A coronation is usually a once-in-a-lifetime experience for any citizen of a monarchy, so Bhutan was pulling out all the stops to prepare for this event. During our visit, we saw people throughout the country building, paving, and widening roads, as well as painting houses—at least the side of the house seen from the road—in preparation for the new king's coronation and the expected influx of visitors.

I felt fortunate to have this rare opportunity to visit Bhutan but had no idea that we would be there at such a crucial time in its democratization. This became one of those coincidences that make birding trips so full of surprises. Oh yes, and I also planned on seeing as many of Bhutan's 670 recorded species of birds as possible.

A chilly morning breakfast at Bhutan's Chele La *mountain pass.*

CHAPTER I

A Unique and Gentle Country

Blazing white, snow-covered peaks of the legendary Himalayan Mountains spread in every direction below our plane. Our destination, Bhutan, is situated on the edge of this massive mountain range, the natural border that separates the Tibetan Plateau from the Indian subcontinent.

After two days of travel from Portland, Oregon, and one day for me to acclimate in New Delhi, my next stop was Bhutan, a remote country that had called to me for years. Our tour guide, Richard Webster, had taken nine of us birders from various parts of the United States on a half-day birding jaunt near New Delhi that whetted our appetites for the long-awaited tour to Bhutan. At last, we were on the final leg of our trip, high above the Himalayan Mountains.

Though I had no idea if April was the right time of year for bird migrations, I scanned the clouds below us looking for moving dots that might be birds. I had read in *Audubon,* the National Audubon Society's magazine, that mountain climbers in the Himalayas have found the bodies of Bar-Headed Geese at very high altitudes. This is proof that they fly through the Himalayan Range while migrating between India and their nesting grounds in Tibet. One theory posits that they usually fly at night. Still, I hoped. *Maybe they didn't all fly by night and maybe this is the right season,* I mused, as I peered downward.

After our three-hour flight, we descended into Paro International Airport located in a deep valley just above 7,300 feet in altitude. The plane bucked and jerked in the rough air that funneled down between the surrounding mountains, some as high as 18,000 feet. We flew so close to local houses that I thought we might be landing in their fields! My heart pounded as we approached the small airport, which may possibly be the most challenging in the world. Later, I read that as of 2011 only eight pilots had been certified to fly into Paro. That, in itself, would have made this trip exciting. I couldn't help but think, *What if all eight of the pilots got the flu at the same time?*

We landed safely and I was grateful to finally set foot in remote Bhutan. I grinned at the others and did a little celebratory wiggle. *At last our birding adventure begins!*

Off to a Great Start

The country requires a Bhutanese cultural guide to accompany all groups visiting Bhutan, so our official Bhutanese guide, Pema, met us at the airport. He would turn out to be a great resource during the long drives when we plied him with questions about Bhutan, its people, and the culture. I am sensitive about asking questions that could be culturally offensive, but I soon learned that Pema almost always gave us informed and polite answers. I even learned that his name, Pema, is a gender-neutral name in Bhutan. My uninformed impression of Bhutan as an isolated country ruled by a monarchy forever, soon changed dramatically, thanks to Pema.

That first night we check into the Dechen Hill Resort in Paro and I climbed into my soft bed and pulled the comforter up to my chin. The gentle patter of rain on the tin roof was relaxing after the long trip. With a long exhale and sigh, I welcomed myself to Bhutan and fell into a deep sleep. But for my two sleeping pills, I would have dressed and undressed in my mind all night long.

A hammering downpour on the tin roof woke me from my happy slumber a few hours later. *My first night in Bhutan,* I thought. *Oh dear, birds don't like rain any more than I do. They'll probably hole up, so we'll have to as well—a fine start. Garumph!*

Despite the rain, I was pumped and ready to explore Bhutan. At dinner the night before, Richard told us to put on all our warm clothes in the morning. "It will be cold on the mountain pass in the pre-dawn hours," explained Richard. "Before daylight we will drive up to *Chele La* at 12,000 feet. 'La' means 'pass' in Dzongkha. The target birds to see at *Chele La* will be two spectacular pheasants."

Richard's description of the pheasants defied belief. I couldn't wait!

From experience, I knew that I would not be able to warm myself by walking since birdwatching is often a static sport. Bhutan was my first test of packing lightly for a three-week trip while still having enough warm clothing for cold weather. If I had spent half the time learning about the birds rather than worrying about what clothing to bring, it would have served me better overall. As I lay awake in the middle of the night, once again I reviewed my clothing; I figured the next day would test my fussing. Anyone can pack for the tropics, but birding in snow, rain, and heat is the real challenge. Still new to international birding, I had yet to experience both extremes on the same trip. Eventually, I did fall back to sleep.

In the morning, I awoke before my 5 o'clock alarm. I heard no wind or rain. When I pulled back the curtains in my room, shimmering stars blanketed the sky dome. I thought, *Ahhh, a good day for birds.*

I donned my layers: long underwear, field pants, rain pants, large shoes to accommodate the two pairs of warm socks, a T-shirt, light fleece shirt, heavy fleece jacket, and a rain jacket. A fleece hat and wind-breaking gloves completed my ensemble. Fat as the Michelin tire man, I grabbed my binoculars and headed out the door to my new adventure. Once outside, I inhaled the bracing mountain air. It was definitely cold!

We all met in the lodge for an early morning snack of coffee, tea, and biscuits. Immediately, I realized I shouldn't have put on *all* my clothes. To avoid suffocating, I peeled off half my layers, counting them so

I wouldn't leave anything behind when we headed to the bus. I wasn't alone in my miscalculation. Jackets, scarves, and hats covered the empty chairs around our long table. After tea and biscuits, I grabbed my heap of clothing and headed to the bus with the others, and then off we drove into the still, black morning.

Some people snoozed on the way to our first high altitude pass, but I didn't want to miss a thing. Silhouettes of evergreen trees emerged as the stars melted into the sky with the first hint of dawn. In time, the sleepers awakened and as the bus ground up the steep and curvy road, we all slowly and eagerly arranged ourselves to peer out the bus's front window. We wanted to catch whatever might appear in the headlights: bats, night birds, or nocturnal mammals.

As we ascended the mountain, a light snow covered the paved road and turned to slush under the bus's tires. Fortunately, we had a careful driver who down-shifted for traction and continued chugging upward. Richard murmured, "This chill will give us better birding than usual. The birds will drop down the mountains to escape the cold higher up."

Oh, boy. Lucky me.

Then the surprise!

Birding at 12,000 Feet

The bus slammed to a halt as a flash of red disappeared over the lip of the heavily forested road. The driver whispered, "Blood Pheasant." Motor off, he added, "He will return. There is no hunting in this country, so they are not afraid."

Giddy with anticipation, eyes riveted on the edge of the road, all ten wide-awake birders silently waited. Suddenly, a deep red bird's head popped into view and looked around. Then, a stunning bird marched into full view—a male pheasant in glorious breeding plumage. Washes of crimson flowed down his creamy chest and under his long tail. A black frame surrounded his solid red face and the soft grey of his back had creamy speckles. What a gorgeous bird!

The haughty blood pheasant looked us over as he considered his next move. A brown female with a grey crest and nape followed him onto the road. Two more females joined them. They waited for his lead, but they were in no hurry. So, for several minutes we took in every detail of these breathtaking birds. This was one of those experiences that I wanted to last forever. I forgot to breathe. A few minutes later, he turned and disappeared off the edge of the road and the magic passed.

It was only the first day of our birding adventure and I already knew this would be a great trip. The spectacular scenery we saw as we flew into Bhutan, along with observing this magnificent bird, was a fabulous beginning to our birding tour in Bhutan. *Wow! What next?*

I savored my view of the blood pheasants as the bus resumed its climb along the fog-shrouded road. Approaching *Chele La,* the headlights illuminated a fluttering, red-and-blue checkered tablecloth covering a long table. A blue tent stood next to the table on the right side of the road. After reassuring myself that my eyes were not playing tricks, I realized that the brown faces split by big grins and peeking around the flap of the tent were our support crew. They had spent the night at the pass so they could set up our first breakfast without delay. Boot prints in the inch-thick layer of late spring snow showed they had already been busy.

Richard stepped off the bus while the rest of us stayed warm inside for a few more minutes as we prepared ourselves for the crisp morning. The Bhutanese crew of six emerged from their cook-stove-heated refuge to greet Richard, familiar to them from previous trips. The men were not warmly dressed, so after a quick reunion they dove back into the toasty tent to prepare our breakfast while we looked for early birds in the dawn's first light.

Behind the cook tent white clouds obscured any possible view. A chorus of snapping from across the road drew my attention. The stiff wind pushed swirls of fog up from the valley, making strings of Buddhist prayer flags stand out straight. Mountain passes in Bhutan are choice spots for small forests of the skinny, flag-covered poles, honoring the death of someone dear, or marking a special holiday. Until the prayer flags deteriorate, the wind sends their good wishes into the universe. Many of the flags were only rags, but they continued to release their messages.

We began our search for birds that thrive high in the rugged mountains. All of us moved at a slow stroll, listening for rustling, cheeps, or songs, and watching for the flash of body parts—maybe a tail or an eye. The birds became more active as the light grew stronger.

Birding was slow going in the cold of 12,000 feet and we hoped we would see more birds down the hillside. Despite my many layers of clothing, I had a difficult time keeping warm. One of my companions who wore less than I did, seemed to shiver, but she never complained, so I just put any whiny thoughts out of my head.

After half an hour, everyone was getting a bit icy and we'd seen the expected birds within a quarter mile of the summit, mostly smaller forest birds like the Coal Tit, which I first thought was a chickadee with a crest. It is a common resident of Bhutan and likes the Bhutan Fir and Himalayan Hemlock trees. We saw a Goldcrest, a yellowish warbler, and the Alpine Accentor, a rugged bird that thrives on open alpine slopes. The Collared Blackbird was among the easier ones to identify with a name that actually reflects what the bird looks like, contrary to many bird names.

Breakfast had to wait while we returned to the bus and drove back down the mountain a short way, hoping the full light of day would reveal more pheasants. On a loop of the road, we disembarked to scan an abandoned field below us. Richard spotted two Himalayan Pheasants meandering in the snow, relatives of the blood pheasants we saw on the way up. They pecked here and there, finding seeds or bugs, or bits of lichen, their favorite food.

Richard and two other birders, who had brought their spotting telescopes, assembled them to give us a closer view. When it was my turn at a telescope, I caught glimpses of the iridescent green, copper, and purple of the male Himalayan pheasant, but I couldn't say for certain that I saw the spatulate-tipped crest that Richard described. The details of the drab females were more of a challenge and I could not pick out their smaller crests because their heads were usually down. However, I was satisfied because I did get a good look at the male pheasant and a sufficient look at the females. Of course, the hardcore birders among us had higher standards and wanted to see much more of the bird. One of them wanted to see every field mark clearly. Another birder wanted to verify that he could identify the birds on his own. I wondered how many birds this birder had seen on trips that he refused to count.

Every birder is free to construct his or her own standards for what constitutes a "good enough view" in order to count the bird among those seen for a personal life list. Most birders do keep a list of birds they have observed, even if it is not the focus of their trip. Others will spend enormous amounts of money and time to find a single bird they haven't seen. Not me. I'm easy. Someone says that's a particular bird, I believe it, and I enjoy the sight.

My stomach grumbled and the others seemed to have had their fill of the magnificent pheasants for the moment—if that was possible.

Breakfast in the Mountains

Returning to *Chele La,* we had a few minutes to look for a private bush before breakfast. In the entire three weeks in Bhutan, we would only see one public restroom and it was locked, reserved for the king when he traveled. It was still early in the morning and no vehicles had passed, so the women chose to go down the road a way and around the corner from the tent. I followed. We squatted in the shallow drainage ditch and hoped for privacy. The eerie view made the risk worthwhile. Hints of sun kissed the fog-shrouded treetops. By the time we headed back up the road to the camp, the clouds seemed to be lifting. While the temperature may not have been below freezing, the brisk wind increased the wind chill and the cold had stiffened our fingers. Back at the tent, the crew had filled a five-gallon canister with heated water for hand washing. The warm water dribbling on my chilly fingers felt divine.

Since I knew I would not get my favorite cup of French press coffee, I got creative with the hot drink options: There was a mix of choices, including Nescafé, Milo, and a chocolate and malt powder mix, plus additional cocoa powder, sugar, tea, and warmed or powdered milk. It didn't matter to me what I had in my cup as long as it was hot and sweet, just what my chilled body needed. Clasping our hot cups to keep our hands warm, we all anxiously waited for our first roadside meal. We stamped our feet to the rattle of the prayer flags, trying to return a bit of feeling to our frozen toes.

At first, I was reluctant to sit at the beautifully set table, complete with a tablecloth. It seemed so decadent. The scene reminded me of something I'd seen in movies where members of the Victorian British upper class sat at a formally set table in a remote field, their staff ready to serve. I couldn't help but think, *Tablecloths, cutlery, linen napkins, and wine glasses at a 12,000-foot mountain pass?*

Well, we did not quite rise to the level of British royalty—no wine glasses or formal dress—but it still was far from being a rugged picnic. Lovely table or not, I envied the crew staying warm inside the cook tent.

Our Bhutanese guide, Pema, wore a short-wrapped robe and knee socks that morning, a bit like a Scottish bagpipe player. His outfit seemed rather skimpy at that high altitude with the wind blowing, especially since Pema had worn Western clothes, pants and a shirt, the day before. Until I knew him better, I didn't feel comfortable asking him about the difference in his attire that day.

In the meantime, we talked about the British influence in Bhutan. I was curious because when I lived in East Africa, the colonial British influence surrounded us and not always in a positive way. Many programs had been instituted to help the Africans by building schools, clinics, and infrastructure. I noticed the arrogance of a few whites who had lived in Africa for years. They believed Africans were "lazy, dishonest, and stupid," and would say so. However, that was not my experience. The African girls I taught were bright, curious, and lively, making my Peace Corps experience a delight.

Pema told us that British explorers had passed through Bhutan in the 19th century to gain access to Tibet, but did not linger. About that time, The British

East India Company, which had become influential in India, had been instrumental in settling border disputes between outlying regions of India and their neighbors, including Bhutan, at least temporarily, to protect what they considered their territory.

With effort, Bhutan maintained its independence until the Chinese invaded neighboring Tibet in 1950. The shadow of the growing Chinese threat motivated Third King Jigme Dorji Wangchuck to reach out to other nations in order to strengthen his country's ability to maintain its independence. His son, Jigme Singye Wangchuck, a student in England at the time his father died in 1972, returned home and continued his father's work as king. Fourth King Wangchuck developed and modernized Bhutan at a pace that would preserve the country's culture and traditions. Pema explained the careful development of Bhutan's resources and I found it to be an admirable and thoughtful undertaking.

The men in the cook tent had pulled back the tent flap and inside, the cook crouched at the two-burner, propane camp stove, stirring eggs in a giant skillet. His helper turned the toasting bread while other workers waited to serve the food and later, clear the dishes. While they waited, they sat in the rear of the warm cook tent, nursing their tea.

Rare Opportunities

Most birding trips to Bhutan occur in the spring because the wildflowers are in bloom and the birds are in breeding plumage and are more approachable.

Much of the snow had melted by the time we arrived for our April trip. Summer monsoons in June, July, and August make travel in Bhutan even more difficult than usual for any travel. The all-male crew that worked with our tour group regularly hosts birding groups for six weeks in the spring, and again in the fall. They are accustomed to loading the same gear on horses to support the trekking parties that come after the rains and before the snow. Key positions on the crew were the cook, the driver, and the camp boss. The other three helpers set up camp, broke it down, and assisted where needed.

Because of the country's inaccessibility and the relatively high tour cost that includes a mandatory government fee of $250 per person, per day, Bhutan is not overrun with tourists at any time of year. However, the Bhutanese who can get jobs working as guides for visiting birders, earn good wages relative to that of most workers in Bhutan.

The sun burned off the last of the fog and the wind died to a gentle zephyr when we sat down for breakfast. I put aside my imperialist reservations about eating in such high style on a mountain pass, and listened to my growing appetite. Bright sunlight sparkled from the snow-covered mountaintops as numerous and jumbled as waves in a roiled ocean. I tuned out the friendly chatter and drank in the breathtaking beauty surrounding me. In the midst of my reverie, a huge bowl of hot oatmeal appeared in front of me.

It was just the beginning of our first full day in Bhutan, and already I was thrilled beyond my greatest imaginings. After breakfast, we climbed on our bus sated and ready for the day to unfold.

The information sign at Chele La.
Four thousand meters equals 13,123 feet.

Pema, our Bhutanese cultural guide,
wore his traditional dress called a gho *to visit a* dzong.

CHAPTER 2

On the Rough Road to Thimphu

We all knew from the morning briefing that after birding at the higher altitudes we would return to the Paro Valley for more birding, then lunch and a drive to Thimphu, the capital of Bhutan. This was another full day, as usual, on a birding trip.

"Our drive to Thimphu will be interesting," Richard told us. Whenever I hear the word "interesting," I always consider that a warning, so I prepared for the details.

"As you know, the only international airport in Bhutan is in Paro," Richard continued. "The road to Thimphu and the rest of Bhutan is thirty-two miles long and it runs through a very steep and narrow canyon. The one-lane, unpaved road clings to a steep canyon wall and there is no alternative route." He paused for moment, then added, "We won't know how long the trip will actually take because that road is being widened to accommodate the extra traffic for the coronation ceremony of Fifth King Jigme Khesar Namgyel Wangchuck."

Richard looked toward Pema to make sure he had gotten all the names right, and then continued. "He became king last December after his father abdicated. I'll let Pema tell you more about that, but you should know that we have to be at the starting point at 3:30 this afternoon in order to get through today, so Pema and I will be keeping a close eye on the time."

I tried not to worry, but I did glance at my watch several times that day. After breakfast, we bussed back down the mountain to look for more birds. Our bus was the familiar twenty-person vehicle similar to ones used on other birding trips, comfortable and dependable. We stopped along the way at promising birding sites, shedding layers of clothing as we dropped in elevation and as the day warmed. Before long, the heavy-duty support truck passed us with all the equipment packed and tied down under a blue plastic tarp in the back. Three men sat atop the load in their down jackets and flip flops, singing and waving. Their boots, tied together by the laces, swung from the side of the truck. The men only used boots for the colder places, and preferred to wear flip-flops, or running shoes.

At noon, we rounded a corner to discover our checkered tablecloth again at another scenic spot on a little hill. Climbing off the bus into pleasantly warm air, we trudged up the grassy slope to our table. Halfway there, an arbor of branches decorated with freshly cut rhododendrons greeted us. The men had prepared our food in the morning and transported it from the breakfast site in insulated containers, so they had plenty of time to refresh the flowers on the arbor. The men grinned at our surprise and pleasure as we passed under their creation. After a "birdy" morning full of new birds, we tucked into a meal of steamed rice with a sumptuous chicken stew and crisp vegetables.

At our birding stops, we met friendly people walking to or from town, or to their plots of land. They wore a mix of well-worn Western clothes, and functional, traditional wraps. Many wore rubber boots for working in wet fields. Everyone smiled, and a few who spoke English chatted with us. Pema chatted with them as we walked along the river, or in the marshes. They seemed to take us in stride. We weren't the first birding group to pass that way.

Living Standards in Bhutan

When we reached the Paro Valley where we had spent our first night, we encountered our first large farms. Because so much of Bhutan is steep and rocky, farmers work every inch of suitable soil. Only two percent of the land in Bhutan is arable, most of which is located in the foothills below 1,000 feet on the 12-mile strip of land in the south that abuts India. There are also bigger farms in the flat valleys of the larger rivers in the middle mountain area at an elevation of about 1,000 to 2,000 feet. Pema said farmers in the Paro River Valley are well off financially, able to build sturdy, larger houses near their fields. These farmers also own animals, and have access to markets for selling their goods.

We saw tidy farms where the same families and their descendants had tended the land for generations.

The well-constructed farmhouses were whitewashed and had solid wooden windows and doors. The ground level housed the animals, usually sheep, goats, a few cows, and an occasional horse. The family occupied the second level. The roof covered the third level, which was open to the weather. The family used the spacious third floor to thresh and store grains, and to wash and dry clothing. Children enjoyed playing games in the dry, protected area out of the mud and rain.

Later in our tour east of Thimphu, we travelled on a rural part of the main road where houses in the few towns were made of mud and wattle construction topped with tin roofs. Older houses had shingle roofs, each with an array of volleyball-sized rocks placed to secure the shingles in the high winds.

The International Fund for Agricultural Development estimates that more than thirty percent of the people in Bhutan are considered to be financially poor, and most of them live in rural areas. These are people who do not own land and have no other way to make a living, but survive on what they can grow on the decreasing supply of public land. Many are currently receiving help from international agencies to learn marketable skills. Access to healthcare, social services, education, and markets is a challenge, often requiring many hours of walking from the isolated villages.

We noticed phallic carvings jutting out from the corners of most roofs in the town of Paro, which we found delightful. Clearly, this was a cultural blip that we tourists did not understand. Pema had heard the questions often, and easily gave us the backstory.

"There are phallic paintings inside and outside the houses," Pema explained. "This custom originated when a *dzong* (a distinctive type of fortress found in Buddhist countries) was built near Punkha to honor Drukpa Kunley, a 15th century monk known as the "Mad Saint" who loved women and wine. The people believe that these phallic symbols drive away the evil eye and gossip."

This information certainly tweaked our prudish view of such a public display, and lively comments circulated around the group. I love this type of cultural experience that challenges my own customs and beliefs.

Driving Over the Construction Site

We arrived at the bridge over the Paro River (*Paro Chhu*) well before 3:30 and I thought we could relax, knowing we would make it to Thimphu that day. I was wrong. The drive was not relaxing.

As we waited at the bridge, Pema gave us a preview of what we would face on the next leg of our trip along this "interesting" one-lane road. "To widen such a con-stricted road, the mountain must be blasted away," Pema explained. "The rubble falls onto the existing road and some into the canyon. The workers must clear a path for traffic as quickly as possible, but it usually takes an hour or so before they can allow a pulse of traffic to pass. Then, traffic from the other end must come this way. You can see this is quite a project."

As he talked, we could see across the river to where huge construction machinery gnawed at an enormous mound of rubble, filling trucks that also had to use the road we were waiting to travel. *Wow, that's a mess!* I thought.

Obviously, this could be done, so I tried to relax and trust that we would make it to Thimphu to continue our tour. *It had started with such lovely birds, mountain scenery, and unusual houses and people,* I told myself. *Surely, this would continue after only a brief delay.*

We had more to learn about roads in Bhutan. While we waited, Pema gave us some background on Bhutan's basic, but difficult road system. For many years, the only way to get to Thimphu from India was by trail from the Indian border. The trek of 130 miles took six days by foot, mule, or horse. In 1961, Third King Wangchuck directed the Bhutan government to develop and oversee the country's First Five-Year Development Plan, which included road construction as a priority, along with building clinics, schools, and markets. India paid for most of the new construction and by 1962 Bhutan had completed the first 109 miles of paved road, which was described as a jeep trail, at best.

"Something you might find interesting is that the king also had to introduce the wheel to people accustomed to carrying bundles on their backs walking up and down the steep terrain," noted Pema. "Wheels are only useful on roads, most of which had yet to be built in Bhutan, and once built, they often washed out. And that is still true today."

We all gasped at that concept of "discovering the wheel in Bhutan." By the mid 1970s, the Bhutanese had constructed just under a thousand miles of paved roads with thousands of manual laborers doing most of the work.

After about half an hour of waiting, traffic started moving and we crossed the bridge. In construction areas where the temporary road had been hastily created that day, our small bus crawled along in the line of vehicles that inched through, and over, piles and pits of dirt and rock. At one point, the truck in front of us tipped so far to the left side that I feared it would topple over, and possibly end up in the canyon. Thankfully, it didn't. None of the vehicles in our line got stuck, but I wondered if the waiting laborers watching our passage might have to lend a hand if that did happen. At times, we were so close to the edge of the cliff, I had a clear view of the river far below. I tried to have faith that we would not topple over the side. Personally, I believe that if I don't name something, it doesn't exist. However, I noticed that the normally chatty birders on the bus were unusually quiet. We did glimpse a few birds down by the river. It was a small comfort to us because they were impossible to identify at such a distance.

The bus crept further east toward the heart of Bhutan, and we knew more fabulous birding awaited us once we got past this unbelievable stretch. I was so intent on each hair-raising moment that I forgot we would have to return along this same route. After an hour, the hastily built, temporary track seemed to improve. Finally, the road split and some traffic continued southwest to India. We followed the vehicles that turned left to cross another high bridge over the merged rivers, and headed northeast toward Thimphu, Bhutan's capital. Fortunately, the road improved because the hillsides were less formidable, and the roadbed was packed and ready for paving.

About six miles from Thimphu, we encountered the future: a paved, two-lane expressway that we sped along into the city. That stretch of road from Paro to Thimphu was the only place in the whole country where we saw any heavy, road-construction machinery. Thousands of manual laborers built the remaining roads by hand.

Government Uniforms in the City

En route to Thimphu, we had more time to question Pema. One of my more pressing questions was, "Given the chilly temperatures at the mountain pass this morning, why are you wearing only a short wrapped robe and knee socks?"

I knew he must have a secret since this was his country. Pema explained that he wore his *gho* (pronounced go), the traditional men's robe, because it was the required men's dress in Thimphu and in all public places. "Our Fourth King Jigme Singye Wangchuck continued the policies of his father to modernize and democratize the country, but he saw the risk of losing what made Bhutan the country that he and all the citizens loved."

Pema continued, "So in 1989, with the consent of his advisors, Fourth King Wangchuck reinforced the traditional dress and behavior code, called *Driglam Namgha*. These traditions had lost favor with many of the people in the past, but the king thought it was important to revive this tradition in order to preserve and strengthen the Bhutanese culture as the country evolved." Pema motioned to his outfit. "Now, the Bhutan government requires all men who work in government offices or schools to wear the *gho*. In addition, men are required to wear this traditional Bhutanese garb on formal occasions and in the towns like Thimphu."

Ever willing to question, I asked Pema how he felt about that.

"Oh, I like it even though it sometimes is a bit inconvenient," Pema admitted. "This morning I had to wear long underwear under my *gho* to stay warm, and I rubbed my hands a lot to keep them warm. Some of the younger people were beginning to fall away from our traditions, and I didn't like that. I'll show you later how to behave at a *dzong*."

A *gho* can be made of any material and the robe hangs to mid-calf. A wide woven sash called a *kera* is wound around the waist and the fabric of the robe is pulled up over it so the hem hangs to knee length. This forms a pocket above the sash that is very handy for carrying things. We saw some men in Thimphu who carried so much stuff in the fold they looked pregnant.

Because all Bhutanese men had to wear their *gho* to official offices, and to monasteries as a sign of respect and an indication of their rank, we learned that a pair of quality, knee-high socks is a most appreciated gift for a Bhutanese man.

"What about the women?" I asked.

"The formal attire for women who work for the government includes a *toego,* a short, open jacket, a *wonju,* which is a blouse, and a *kira,* a floor-length, brightly colored panel of cloth that wraps around their waist." Pema added, "You will not see many women in this attire in Thimphu since the men dominate the official government positions."

Even the young people in Thimphu, who love to watch television and dress in modern clothes in their free time, are happy to don their traditional dress as required for school and work in spite of the delicious attraction to Western styles.

Later, when we traveled to remote towns far beyond city limits, fewer people wore the traditional garb. Many men wore well-used Western-style pants and jackets, and women wore lightweight wrapped skirts and simple tops. Given the choice myself if I were a man, I would take the pants over the *gho* the men wore. I imagined those winds rushing up underneath their robes would freeze everything.

Pema's information about different dress codes for his country fascinated me, and it piqued my interest even further. I asked, "How did such a dress evolve in a country with weather as violent and cold as Bhutan's?"

He did not know.

Later, when I returned home, I researched this question further. I learned that the wrap-type of clothing was the first used in every culture since weaving a flat piece of cloth developed early, and that trousers evolved only after people began to ride horses. When I learned this, I was chagrined at my cultural bias and disconnect from the obvious.

Buddhists & Animals

Buddhists revere all life and will go to great lengths to preserve the life of every living creature. Unfortunately, problems can arise. For example, Thimphu is overrun with feral dogs. Tourists feel threatened by the larger ones and complain about the nocturnal barking. Residents feed many of the dogs that settle into the neighborhood for the convenient meals. Several solutions have been tried; retirement homes and spay/neuter programs have proved inadequate against the dogs' persistent breeding. Natural selection would limit the dog population, but as long as food is available, the dogs will breed to capacity.

Even at our tent camp at 10,000 feet, a small pack of dogs wandered around our tents and erupted into a loud chorus of barking and howling that scared me out of a sound sleep. I had not expected to encounter dogs in such a remote place, but thought they might be hunting the reported rare mountain bears that roamed the area. But no such luck. They were farm dogs patrolling their territory, surprised at our intrusion. I must admit the dogs' presence deflated my feeling of pleasant isolation that night.

Exploring Thimphu

In the waning daylight, we set out to see a bit of Thimphu, the largest city in Bhutan, and the center for most of the political/administrative activities. Earlier, when we turned off the rough road from Paro and onto the new road, we had passed newer developments built to accommodate the recent influx of people. Government changes in 2007 had called for more administrators, and Thimphu's population had expanded to about 66,000 residents. As of 2017, the population is about 104,000 people. Later, we learned that too few jobs are available to the rural people who migrate from their home valleys. As a result, Thimphu and the other towns are overwhelmed with the needs of a growing population.

In the city's center, the buildings were primarily of traditional construction with lots of heavy wood beams and white painted stucco, accented with colorful decorations around the windows, doors, and under the eaves. Frequently, we saw rosy-cheeked locals spinning Buddhist prayer wheels placed in open spaces throughout the town. Small roofs protected the prayer wheels, but not the people who used them in the rain.

We ducked into a few shops, looking for indigenous crafts, but we soon lost our energy. The altitude of 7,656 feet still took some acclimation. In addition, it had been a long day since our pre-dawn tea and snack, so we were all feeling sluggish. An early night was in order for all of us. The next day would be another one full of birds and more surprises.

Punakha Dzong. *The bridge was replaced between the visible buttresses soon after our visit.*

CHAPTER 3

Punakha Dzong and Buddhism

On the West Coast of the United States where I live, any structure standing for 100 years is considered old. Imagine how I felt when we visited some of Bhutan's traditional *dzongs* (pronounced zong), first built in the 12th century. These are enormous stone structures built as fortresses and administrative centers, often on top of existing temples, and later used as fortresses to defend the former Buddhist kingdoms of Bhutan, Tibet, and Himalayas in the 1600s. When I finally stood next to one, I was in awe of the massive towering exterior walls, surrounding complex courtyards, temples, monks' living quarters, and administrative offices.

Pema, who answered questions about all things Bhutanese, brimmed with information about the history, construction, and use of the *dzongs*. In the early 1600s, the Tibetan Buddhist lama Zhabdrung Ngawang Namgyal unified the warring tribes into a nation-state now known as Bhutan. He wanted to create a distinct Bhutanese culture separate from Tibet, so he commanded that more of the massive *dzongs* be built.

Today, trekkers can find the remote *dzongs* clinging to impossible cliffs and other locations strategically chosen to defend against warring neighbors. .

Morning Birding

On our fourth day of birding, we arose before dawn to catch the early birds as usual. We were staying in the town of Punakha located fourteen miles northeast of Thimphu on the map, twice as far by the twisty road. Punakha was the original capital of Bhutan and home to one of the country's oldest and most beautiful *dzongs*. We passed the massive whitewashed walls of Punakha Dzong on our way out of town. Constructed on a point of land at the confluence of two rivers, the *dzong* shone in the first rays of the morning sun. I eagerly anticipated our visit to Punakha Dzong after our morning birding.

We drove slowly up the Pho Chhu Valley for about two hours, stopping frequently as the birds woke up and began moving. In the morning shadows of the steep-sided valley, we encountered a variety of birds, including the hard-to-find Tawny Fish-owl, Slaty-bellied Tesia, Bay Woodpecker, a beautiful blue Verditer Flycatcher, the impressive Slender-billed Scimitar-babbler, noisy flocks of the Nepal Fulvetta, and a Maroon Oriole. At our lunch stop, we enjoyed a shimmering blanket of yellow and black butter-flies clustered at the edge of a small stream, sipping the moisture from the wet sand. On birding trips, I always love that we see so much more than the birds we are seeking.

Pema scanned the river as we drove back down the valley. Suddenly, he raised his voice to the driver who slammed on the brakes. He pointed to two tall birds standing at the edge of the fast flowing water. Richard jumped off the bus, took a look through his binoculars, and turned to us with a big smile on his face.

"Good spot, Pema! White-bellied Herons, also called Imperial Herons," he said as we all positioned ourselves for a good view of the long-necked birds. Their grey bodies disappeared into the grey river rocks, making Pema's discovery even more incredible. "These herons used to breed in this valley years ago, but now they are endangered and hard to find, especially at this time of year," Richard explained. "I can see a bit of breeding plumage, so maybe they are nesting in the area again. The best estimates are that only 250 to 1,000 white-bellied herons remain."

Punakha Dzong

Thrilled with a great morning of birding, our next stop was just as exciting for me—visiting a *dzong*, one of the iconic structures so key to Bhutan's history. My first impression as we walked up to Punakha Dzong was, *What a massive structure!* The monastery fortress built more than five centuries earlier, was heavy and thick in its architectural appearance. It had formidable tilted walls that made it look totally impregnable, which was the point.

Chhu means river, and the Punakha Dzong is located at the confluence of the *Mo Chhu* (Mother River) and the *Pho Chhu* (Father River). It is close to the town of Punakha, and is the second oldest, and the second largest *dzong* in Bhutan. Punakha Dzong is one of six *dzongs* in Bhutan still used as a monastery and it is considered one of the most majestic. Until the mid-1950s, Punakha Dzong was the seat of the Bhutanese government, and today it is still the winter residence of the *dratshang,* the central Buddhist monk body.

In 1637, Shabdrang Ngawang Namgyal, who first united the fiefdoms in Bhutan, ordered the construction of the Punakha Dzong on the site of a smaller structure built in 1326 that housed a statue of Buddha. Since then, Punakha Dzong has survived fires, earthquakes, and flooding from the two rivers. The repairs from a 1994 flood have returned much of the *dzong* to its original state. The whitewashed, beaten mud, and stonewalls contrasted with the *dzong's* dark wooden beams, window frames, and roof.

Pema wore an especially formal *gho* for the day and had brought a white scarf for his visit to the *dzong.* Every Bhutanese person must wear a scarf indicating his or her status when visiting the *dzongs.* Colored scarves are reserved for royals, Buddhist ranks, and government officials. Everyone else wears a white scarf. Before leaving our bus for the *dzong,* Pema draped his scarf across one shoulder and carefully fastened it in a particular manner that looked more like a fold than a knot.

We approached the *dzong* via a short suspension bridge over the *Mo Chhu,* a temporary bridge that replaced the older one ripped from its foundations during the 1994 flood. Stepping carefully across the uneven planks, I felt anxious suspended over the wildly rambunctious water thrashing close to my feet. The bridge felt quite steady as I crept along and my confidence increased. I paused in the middle of the bridge, savored the thrill of danger, and recalled other hanging bridges we had seen on our trip that clung to the lips of deep canyons. I thought, *Should the worst occur, I would not have a long drop. I would, however, have a rather rough ride in the water.*

With that thought, I picked up my pace to get off that bridge.

A couple of older men in faded clothing loitered at the gate that pierced the ten-foot-high perimeter wall. They watched the monks, tourists, and civil servants coming and going. We all greeted the men with a smile and passed through the gate.

Inside the outer wall, the main buildings towered above us. We paused to appreciate the quiet well-tended gardens with only a few strolling monks and their visitors. Designed as a fort, there is no ground-level entrance to the *dzong* itself, which would deter a surprise attack. We had to walk up a long flight of steep steps leading to an open roofed foyer. Each stair step was much higher than our standard stairs and any enemies trying to rush the place would be winded by the time they reached the top!

While we listened to Pema offer details on the *dzong*, I noticed three high-school-age monks with shaved heads and red robes lounging on the top steps, possibly taking a break from their studies. I pointed my camera toward them and one held up his hand to signal no photo. *Oops! Too late!* I thought as I snapped a photo. They must see many tourists taking photographs, so I felt a bit ashamed that I had not respected their monastic privacy. We were, after all, visiting a religious place of education and worship, not a tourist attraction.

We struggled up the steep steps to the entry foyer where bright, colorful murals depicting the life of Buddha and various deities covered the walls. Carved and painted intricate detail covered every wooden surface. As Pema explained the figures, he spun one of the two large prayer wheels that flanked the entry door. The mantra in each wheel invokes benevolent attention, and each rotation of the wheel spreads spiritual blessings and well-being.

The Monks' Daily Ceremony

We entered an inner courtyard where painted flowers and leaves, delicate Bhutanese script, animals, and gilded garlands decorated the interior walls, posts, and beams. Discrete wall niches displayed small replicas of Buddha. All the color and texture overwhelmed me, so I turned with relief to the ancient, thick-leaved almond tree in the center of the courtyard. House sparrows chirping in the old tree helped ground me.

From the sunny courtyard, Pema invited us to observe the monks' daily afternoon ceremony. Another set of steep stairs made me wonder if they were built with a high rise to give the monks exercise as they went about their daily activities. As we approached the next set of stairs, we could hear the deep moans of horns, crisp drumbeats, and bright cymbal clashes. The heavy wood interior, darkened by centuries of incense burning, absorbed much of the light that entered through small openings high in the roof. The dim light added an element of mystery to the interior.

We crossed the open floor of the balcony and peered over the railing at the scene below. Perhaps 50 monks draped in cranberry-colored robes sat like red pyramids on the uncluttered wooden floor. The horns boomed their reverberating note again from beneath my feet. Moving to a better spot, I found the horn players sitting against one wall tucked under the balcony, the ten-foot-long wooden and brass horns stretched straight out in front of them. I wondered if that could be what an unwound tuba or sousaphone might look like. It must have taken terrific lung volume to make any sound emerge from those huge instruments, much less the full reverberating sounds that filled the large hall. I got dizzy just thinking about it.

On the platform next to the horns, a chanting monk reverently fingered the ancient book that lay before him, even though he seldom needed to glance at it. Two lines of monks facing one another stretched away from the chanting monk across the hall. Each monk in the front row held a slim pole planted firmly on the floor. At the top of the six-foot-pole a small, flat, two-sided drum swayed a little as a monk beat it with a long drumstick. The drumstick was thin

267

and straight to the upper end and then curved in a crescent so the padded tip struck the drum at a right angle to the head. The ping from the tenor drums balanced the labored, deep notes from the horns. The precision and unity as the drummers responded to the chanting monk fascinated me.

One drumstick did not seem to be in synch with the others. In fact, it seemed the monk holding it was weaving a little, dozing off, perhaps. No one seemed bothered. He jerked awake and joined the others for a few more strikes, then dozed off again. One or two of the others smiled a bit, but no one attempted to wake him. I delighted in this bit of humanness amidst the reverence in this centuries-old ceremony.

Behind each line of drumming monks sat two more red rows of monks. Occasionally, one would get up and walk out. Another would enter, find an unoccupied spot, and settle among his brother monks. Once again, mesmerized by what I saw, questions arose about Bhutan's culture and lifestyle. I wondered, *What can I draw from this? Is this ceremony optional? Do the monks come and go when other duties allow? Do the ones who do not come demonstrate a lack of commitment?*

I moved to the other side of the balcony where an older monk also watched the activities below. When the drumming finished, the monks laid down their drums and sat in silence. After a pause, a young monk with a container full of uncooked grain emerged from a dark door in the wooden wall. He stopped in front of each monk and scooped a handful of uncooked rice into each man's lap. On cue from the reader, each monk pinched a bit of grain and tossed it with a flick of the wrist. Most did so without obvious concern where it landed. Some threw it high into the air, and one of the youngest monks, a teenager, clearly had a target in mind. He grinned broadly after several tosses in a specific direction, though I could not pinpoint the recipient of his attention. I glanced at the elderly monk who had to have seen the antics, but he seemed undisturbed, neither a smile nor a frown. *Did he remember being a boy himself?*

When the raw rice was finished, most of the monks unfolded a white cloth that each one placed in his lap. Two younger monks entered with large pots of boiled white rice, their bare feet shushing as they moved down the line. Stopping in front of each monk, they pushed a small saucepan into the pot and plopped a lump of sticky rice onto the cloth. The recipients knotted their cloths and put them aside. Some monks got more rice than others. Some had not spread their cloth and the providers passed by them. Once again, questions popped into my mind. *What could all this mean?*

I had so many questions: *Was I just reading more than what was intended into a daily activity? Possibly a monk was on a diet? Fasting? Was this voluntary or imposed?*

In the end, my questions faded as even more questions took their place.

What Is, Is

When Pema signaled for us to leave, we descended another set of perilous wooden steps to a smaller courtyard. The steps were higher than I am used to, so I ran my hand along the wall to steady myself.

The ceilings of the halls were very high, so the outside of the building was as tall as a five- or six-story building. Big and small windows with little balconies broke the expanse of white walls. We took some time to appreciate the detailed carvings and paintings on every inch of the wood.

Pema led us across the courtyard to another hall. We could see through a doorway where younger monks gathered. I assumed they had just finished the same ceremony we had witnessed because rice grains remained on the polished floor. Pema indicated we should remove our shoes outside since we were entering the actual hall, not just observing from above. There was no balcony, but the interior was dark and cavernous like the other one.

As Pema lectured on the history and the significance of more paintings of Buddha and the deities that covered the walls, I watched the youngest boys clustered to one side of the hall, dressed in the same red robes as the adult monks. Most of them looked between five and twelve years old. An older boy in charge seemed to be lecturing them. Then, he pointed to several boys who grabbed bundles of reeds and swept up the bits of scattered rice. The others milled about, chatting, laughing softly, and watching us. I wondered about the boys' friendly shoving of one another, unseemly for monks, but I guessed they were boys first of all. An older monk sat at the bottom of one of the pillars in the middle of the hall. Was he overseeing the boys? They didn't seem to be paying attention to him, so perhaps he was a keeper of the hall. Observing this brief scenario, I wondered, *Why would boys want to come here? Who were they? Didn't their families miss them? What if they didn't measure up to the rigors of training?*

Pema patiently answered our more practical questions. "Most boys join a monastery around five or six years of age, chosen and encouraged by their families who consider it an honor to have a son in the community. Traditionally, monks have had better access to education than the rest of the population, though that is changing as our schools improve. Monks continue their education into specialties needed by the community."

"Can the boys go home?" I asked.

"The boys visit their families on occasion," explained Pema, "and the families come to the monastery when they are able, though many live too far away. Boys who decide not to stay are allowed to leave, but the family is expected to pay for the training received, which I think must put pressure on the boys to continue."

Pema paused, then added, "One nice thing for the monk's family is his availability when the family needs a blessing. We have a lot of those occasions; weddings, deaths, new babies, opening a new house, even the seasonal changes are all richer when a monk joins the celebrations and offers his blessings."

Then I asked Pema, "The monks spend so much time sitting in meditation, in ceremonies, or in classes. How do they survive the cold and inactivity?"

Pema smiled and waved his hand toward the boys. "The cold temperature is just another challenge to overcome while meditating. Squirming is discouraged. It takes the boys awhile, but they learn to use the discomfort as a way to deepen their practice. They do have a chance to run around during their breaks. The older monks do walking meditations."

The monk I had seen on the balcony appeared later on the steps to the smaller hall, chatting amiably with another monk. At a distance, it looked like he might be carrying a whip, but on closer inspection, the strands were only cotton cloth. Another question for Pema: Was it symbolic?

I thought, *Surely, the monks guided the young miscreants toward appropriate behaviors without coercion in such a gentle practice.*

Pema explained that the Buddhist monks live in the present moment. "What is, is."

So the monks I thought might be judging the younger boys were, in fact, just observing them. Their very presence would be enough guidance for the boys who were learning the gentle lessons of Buddhism.

On the April day we visited, I was comfortable in long sleeves and pants. It was the edge of spring with pleasant weather, but I knew that many days at that high altitude are not warm. We did not see any fireplaces in the *dzong*, though it is possible the living quarters had some source of heat. Maybe the monks bulked up with layers of underclothes in the cold weather, like Pema did when we reached the chilly passes.

I was not tempted to romanticize a life at Punakha Dzong, as I do about some other situations I experience. At 64 years old, I was past the age of entry to commit to a life of austerity, but I respected the men and boys for their choices, and for their contributions to the life of the community. With all the changes as Bhutan continues to move toward modernity, I hoped the spirit of Buddhism would continue to thrive in Bhutan.

The rock-to-gravel work station,
where workers pounded stones into bits.

CHAPTER 4

Hand-Built Roads

On our travels through Bhutan, I became fascinated with the country's road building. Even in 2007, I could see that the challenge of carving roads from the steep mountainsides with poor equipment meant constant maintenance. During our tour, we passed every phase of road development, from construction crews digging the roadbed out of the steep hillside with huge construction machinery to groups of workers digging out the hillside by hand with only one truck to haul rocks.

Until the early 1960s, Bhutanese hauled their heavy loads on networks of steep and narrow paths that had been used for centuries for travel by foot, mule, or horseback. As of 2003, about 5,000 miles of roads had been built with about 3,100 miles of them paved. After years of work to improve old roads and add new ones, in 2006 one-fifth of the population still lived more than a half-day's walk from an all-season road.

Violent storms hammer the hillsides during the rainy season, and slides and erosion are common due to the light soils and poor quality of road construction. Despite all of these challenges, the road building continues.

Slowly, the schools, clinics, markets, and shops have become more accessible.

When we traveled on the steep mountain roads, we could find birds easily by looking down into the crown of the trees below where the birds were active. Occasionally, a battered truck hauling road-building supplies, or a sedan full of people, drove by slowly. Customarily, the occupants smiled and waved when passing tourists and beeped their horn in greeting. We tried to be gracious and could only hope the unexpected blare of the horns hadn't spooked some elusive bird. Some of those roads were lovely with a well-hardened center for the vehicles, while others showed signs of recent repair after a slide.

Making Gravel

One day while birding east of Trongsa in central Bhutan, we strolled along one of the winding roads until about mid-morning. Turning a corner, we walked into an area where landslides had denuded the slopes, but the road was passable and we continued. Soon, we began to hear rhythmic pinging, metal on metal.

Around another corner, in a rare wide spot on the narrow road, we found a camp for road construction workers. They lived in one elongated shelter covered with black plastic for a roof. Next to it, a dozen workers, shaded against the sun, crouched on a one hundred-foot-long heap of small stones piled three- to four-feet high. The workers, mostly women and teens, squatted on top of the pile and bashed larger stones into gravel-sized bits with handheld mallets and chisels.

Across the road from them, two toddlers sat close to their mother while she cracked medium-sized rocks. The younger child played in the dirt while the older one pounded his own little rock with a stick, imitating his mother.

Nearby, another heap of larger rocks awaited them. I never saw anyone using gloves. No one wore eye protection. At home, these safety precautions would be required. The fact that I immediately noted what "was missing," reminded me that this was an example of my own cultural biases and assumptions as well as my concern for what I considered safety precautions. This wasn't an option in Bhutan.

In a lull of activity, Pema told us how Bhutan's poor roads, or lack of roads at all, have been a barrier to good governance, education, health care, and social services, as well as commerce. The Indian government has always supplied skilled Indian crews for road building as a part of the foreign aid it gives Bhutan. In return, Bhutan has awarded most of its construction contracts to Indian companies, not an unusual arrangement in foreign aid agreements. Indian contract workers who do the actual road construction, build temporary shelters out of used lumber, poles, and black plastic on the few shoulders where the roads are wide enough to accommodate them. They live in these makeshift shelters for three or four months, and then return to their homes in India. The downside of this arrangement is that local people never learn how to do the roadwork, a growing problem as labor demands increase.

Gutter Construction

Because the Himalayan mountain range is the youngest in the world, the soil on top is less compact than on older mountains, resulting in frequent slides when rains saturate the soil. Heavy stone gutters run along the uphill side of the mountain roads to collect excess runoff. At the major dips in the road, a culvert collects water so it will cross under the road and run down the slope to prevent erosion.

One day, we walked along a gutter that looked quite new—no weeds in the bottom, or bits of dirt or gravel. Soon, we came upon a crew of six men and women building the continuation of that stone gutter. One laborer far ahead of the others dug out the square ditch four feet across and two feet deep. Behind him was the mason, who was the only person dressed in blue overalls. He lined the bottom and the sides of the gutter with stones from a pile at the side of the road that a supply truck replenished periodically. The mason placed the top row of stones to exactly line up with his tight leveling string. Two women followed him and added smaller rocks between earth and the stones. Behind the women, a worker filled the spaces between the rocks with mortar.

Another laborer hauled water from the streams or rivulets that rolled down every gully. The last man in line mixed the cement and water on a clean spot in the road and filled the gaps between the set rocks. The finished gutter was square inside and big enough to carry large volumes of water to the culverts that another crew built. Later, we watched a team of culvert workers as they constructed the spillways, setting the sizable rocks into almost vertical slopes. I marveled at the entire process and the ingenuity of the workers to build roads with their bare hands.

Some of the splendid birds we saw during that quiet walk included Gray-chinned Minivets, our first Striated Bulbul, my only Brownish-flanked Bush-warbler, the first Gray-cheeked Warbler, our only Broad-billed Warbler, the first Rufous-bellied Niltava, and White-throated Fantail, (which actually does fan its tail), several Golden Babblers and a flock of Streaked Laughingthrush. These last birds travel in flocks and their chattering sounds really do sound like laughing. I smile whenever I remember their intense movements and joyous vocalizations.

Road Scenes

At one stop, I took out my camera and approached a group of workers. They knew what I wanted and paused for a photo without hesitation, pleased that I had taken an interest in them. When I showed them the thumbnail digital image, they grinned with pleasure. In other countries, such an event might evoke demands for money, but these workers thanked me for my attention and then returned to their work.

Another day, one of the small, three-wheeled tractors putt-putted slowly down the road toward us and I did the same "may I take your picture" motions. The driver nodded enthusiastically and an struck a stiff, formal pose. When he saw that the photo included the two people sitting behind him in the tractor box, probably hitchhikers, he motioned for me to take a photo of *just* him and his machine. When I showed him the image, he seemed pleased with that framing.

In several remote places, the one-lane tarmac road had been widened by digging the mountainside shoulder down four inches from the road level, filling the depression with fist-sized rocks, and covering them with dirt. The firm surface supported the infrequent times one vehicle passed another. In addition, free-roaming cattle could graze on the grass that grew from the dirt. It was a creative way to meet the two functions for that portion of the road—pasture and travel surface.

We often encountered cattle strolling along the road, sometimes followed by someone with a long, sturdy stick. Unattended, they roamed the hillsides in search of another blade of grass, creating paths in their wake. I kept an eye out for those paths for times that I might want to get off the road for a moment of relief. It was a risky choice, but with heavier traffic in places and Pema following us, I took it. I did envision someone finding my cold, battered body at the bottom of a gully with my pants wrapped around my ankles. A deep breath quelled my reservations.

Rock Diggers

On another mountain road under repair, we heard the deep clack of heavy rocks colliding. We approached a young man who stood near a loose barrier of large rocks that curved around the bottom of the slope, almost blocking the road. When he saw us, he yelled uphill. A voice drifted down in reply. I wanted to know what they were doing, but nothing happened until we were clear on the other side of their work area and out of the way.

As the birders continued down the road, I held back to watch the workers, fascinated with the road building. The young man on the road shouted uphill again. A large rock, about three feet across, flew out of the bushes, bounced down the slope, and hit the barrier with a clonk. More shouting, and another rock hurtled down the steep slope, but the timing of the bounce caused this one to fly over the barrier, hit on the side of the road, and jump into the void below. The man on the road shouted up and laughed. A loud grunt returned from the bushes.

The uphill man moved into view, dressed in shorts and rubber boots. Next to a large boulder, he picked up a sledgehammer and wacked away, smashing the pieces into a more manageable size for him to kick into a roll. One of the pieces of the boulder refused to move, so he sat down above it and pushed with his feet, grunting and shouting what I can only assume were some colorful words of encouragement. Finally, the stubborn rock loosened up and joined the pile at the bottom. Later, a truck delivered these rocks to the stone bashers we had passed earlier.

Bhutanese workers maintain the roads once Indian crews build them. This is a paying job available for Bhutanese people without land or marketable skills. The government employs more than three people per mile of road. The workers live in government-built, cement-block houses that are sooty from cooking fires.

Several families live in each tiny roadside community. During the dry season, they clear weeds from the hillsides and clean out the gutters to prepare for the rainy season.

When a rockslide blocks a road after days of heavy rain, the first vehicle on the scene from either side returns to the nearest town to report the blocked road. Trucks collect the road workers from their settlements between the towns and deliver them to the blockage. Within an hour of the discovery, workers are attacking the debris with shovels and wheelbarrows. What they lack in heavy equipment they make up for in sheer numbers, and in a relatively short time, the traffic is moving again.

These were good jobs for the workers, but I kept picturing the image of Sisyphus in Greek mythology. For a transgression against the gods, he had to push his boulder up a hill only to have it roll down to the bottom again and again, forever.

Gutter construction on a steep mountain road.

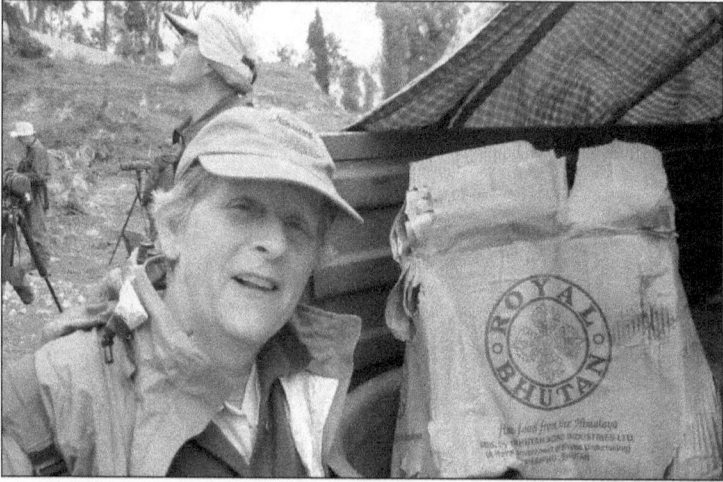

Harriet with a labeled rice bag, proof of her visit.

CHAPTER 5

Gross National
Happiness

On our long drives, Pema talked with us about his country's history and values, and the complexities of modernizing such an insular society. His comments helped me understand Bhutan's unique culture and history.

For centuries, self-sufficient Bhutanese people lived in isolated valleys connected to their fields and other villages only by steep mountain paths. In 1634, Ngawang Namgyal, the Tibetan Buddhist lama and political outcast, unified Bhutan for the first time as a nation-state. He set up a dual system of government and codified a system of laws. After Namgyal's death in 1651 the country struggled for two centuries to maintain the spiritual and administrative systems he had established.

At the end of the 1800s, Ugyen Wangchuck, the Governor of the Province of Trongsa, quelled the nation-state's civil unrest and informally ruled the country for ten years. When the last spiritual leader died in

1903 and no successor could be found, the governors of Bhutan's providences elected Ugyen Wangchuck as their first *Druk Gyalpo,* a title that means Dragon King, and from that time forward, his people have called themselves *Drukpa* or Dragon People.

First King Wangchuck founded a line of benevolent kings who, over many years, have moved Bhutan away from an absolute monarchy in which the king made all decisions. Great Britain was Bhutan's model for a desired democratic constitutional monarchy in which the power of the monarch is limited and balanced by an elected body. In addition, Mahayana Buddhism is the spiritual practice of the kings and of all Drukpas, and the core values of that practice have guided Bhutan's transition to a democracy.

Emerging from Isolation

First King Wangchuck, who ruled from 1907 to 1926, gently improved the infrastructure of his impoverished country by slowly building roads, schools, and health care facilities. Second King Jigme Wangchuck, who was First King Wangchuck's son and successor, received an education in Buddhist literature, English, and Hindi. During Second King Wangchuck's rule from 1926 to 1952, he increased the power of the central government and carefully relaxed Bhutan's isolation by allowing limited relations with the British Raj in India. By the mid-20th century, Bhutan still had no durable roads in large part due to heavy rains and the threat of landslides. In addition, the northern boundary with Tibet had not yet been finalized, and its southern border with

India was still being negotiated after the withdrawal of Great Britain from India in 1948.

The Chinese occupation of Tibet in the 1950s presented a compelling reason for Third King Jigme Dorji Wangchuck, who ruled from 1952 to 1972, to hasten modernization of his country in order to protect its autonomy. However, his desire to build modern Bhutan based on the values of the 16th century Tibetan founders made the transition difficult as Bhutan emerged into the global milieu.

Third King Wangchuck appointed ministers to advise him during the initial transition from the absolute monarchy. At their suggestion in 1953, he established Bhutan's National Assembly, a unicameral body of the people's representatives in order to spread the responsibilities of governing. Final decisions still needed the king's approval. In 1968, this changed so that the National Assembly's decisions did not need the king's approval. In 2007, the establishment of the National Council created a bicameral body for governance like those in Britain and the United States.

Third King Wangchuck's attention to the historic values of Bhutan may have caused him to miss the significance of the increasing number of immigrants settling in the southern region of Bhutan with cultural beliefs that differed from Drukpa.

Immigration Problems in Bhutan

In the early 1900s, the Bhutanese government encouraged immigration from other countries to the arable strip of land on its southern border where few

Drukpas lived. The "people of the south," called the Lhotshampa, established farms and paid taxes that supported early economic development in Bhutan. However, the government forbade the Lhotshampas to settle north of the subtropical foothills, confining them to southern Bhutan.

The Lhotshampa population in Bhutan had never been officially considered part of the Bhutanese population, but by the 1950s the government became concerned about the possible threat from their increasing numbers. As Bhutan matured, the Lhotshampa, along with other residents, benefitted from the expanding availability of government services in education and healthcare. To address the problem of increased migration by the Lhotshampa, Third King Wangchuck established the Citizenship Act of 1958 that declared *only* citizens, not *all* residents of Bhutan, would be eligible to receive government services. Because the concept of citizenship had never been clearly defined, he granted citizenship to anyone with a Bhutanese father. In addition, Lhotshampas who could prove they had lived in Bhutan for at least ten years prior to 1958 and owned agricultural land could become citizens. At the same time, the Bhutanese government banned any further immigration in an attempt to control the increase in the Lhotshampa population. However, lacking any means of enforcement, illegal immigration into Bhutan continued unchecked for many years.

In 1961, Bhutan began to implement the first in a series of five-year-development plans to guide modernization. Over the years, these plans have focused on attainable economic and developmental goals, so the work has been steady but slow. In the 1970s, the Fourth Five-Year Plan included an increased number of construction projects, including roads, bridges, culverts, and other infrastructure. Most Drukpas lacked the construction skills needed to meet the planning objectives, so Bhutan had to open its borders again to workers from India and Nepal eager for the work opportunities. Most workers returned to their homes after the contracts were completed, but many of the Nepalese stayed and easily settled into the Lhotshampa-populated states in southern Bhutan.

In addition, from 1960 to 2017 the population of neighboring Nepal tripled from 10 million to roughly 30 million. Nepal is among the economically poorest nations in the world and its government's weak leadership of its multi-ethnic population has hampered international attempts to develop the country's economy. As a result, migrants continue to leave Nepal seeking better places to live and Bhutan has been one of those destinations.

Deporting Immigrants

In 1985, advisers to Fourth King Jigme Singye Wangcheck alerted him that the government estimated the Lhotshampas comprised about 28 percent of Bhutan's total population. Lacking an official census, other estimates were even higher. The government dealt with this renewed immigrant threat by tightening the requirements for Bhutanese citizenship. New immigration laws required that *both* parents of an applicant had to be Bhutanese—not just the father. If both parents were not Bhutanese, then the applicant had to be fluent in Dzongkha, Bhutan's national language, and had to thoroughly understand Bhutanese customs, which basically meant the customs of the Drukpa. All other immigrants would have to leave the country. In addition, the new immigration requirements stated that anyone who had ever spoken against the king would be deported.

After the king tightened the citizenship rules, officials began the necessary work to enforce them. In 1988, the government initiated a census to clarify population numbers by ethnicity. It is important to note that the census took five years to complete and only took place in southern Bhutan where Lhotshampas live, causing them understandable agitation. To enforce the acceptance of the Drukpa culture in 1989, the king instituted the "One Nation, One People" policy, which required *everyone* to adopt Bhutanese (Drukpa) traditional dress and language. This meant that Lhotshampas had to wear garments not of their tradition and speak a language not their own. School classes in southern Bhutan had to be taught in Dzongkha, and the traditional language of the Lhotshampas, Nepali, could only be spoken at home.

The Lhotshampa leaders tried to get the Bhutanese government to review its policies but to no avail. In 1990, Lhotshampas organized anti-government rallies to get representation in the Bhutanese government, and they demanded citizenship for those without it. The Bhutan government retaliated by cracking down on the Lhotshampa's acts of dissent, forcing more than 100,000 people deemed to be illegal immigrants to leave Bhutan.

Many deported Lhotshampas had lived in Bhutan for generations, so they had no "home" to return to and lived in crowded Nepalese refugee camps. Feeling they had unjustly been deported from Bhutan, they testified to human rights investigators that the Bhutanese examiners freely manipulated the deportation process to meet the desired numbers of deportees. Poorly trained census takers added to Lhotshampas's belief that the Bhutan government's treatment had been riddled with injustice.

When I was on my tour of Bhutan, I was not aware of the political implications surrounding the Lhotshampa issues. However, when a member of our tour group asked Pema about immigration problems in Bhutan, all Pema would say about the expulsion of Lhotshampas in the early 1990s was that "they were illegal." I took what Pema said at face value to avoid sticky political discussions. After all, as a representative of his government, Pema would be expected to give us the official perspective.

It's easy for outsiders to point out what's wrong with a country, but I hesitated to do that especially when my own country also has major ongoing immigration issues. Instead, on the tour I decided to focus on Bhutan's natural beauty, the birding, and the country's fascinating cultural aspects.

Gross National Happiness Index

Bhutan created the First Five-Year Plan for development in 1961, which focused on attainable goals based on the core values of Mahayana Buddhism. In 1972, Fourth King Jigme Singye Wangchuck inspired the concept of Gross National Happiness (GNH) when he declared that happiness was more important than Gross Domestic Product (GDP), the index used by most countries to determine only their economic health.

To support the political transition, the king charged Bhutan's planners to consider the four pillars of GNH when developing subsequent five-year plans: good governance, a sustainable and equitable economy, preservation and promotion of culture, and environmental conservation. For the planning to move forward, the government had to again gather data and then set criteria and methods of measurement. As the work progressed, the king's concept of gross national happiness became measurable and properly named as the Gross National Happiness Index.

In 2001, Fourth King Wangchuck charged the National Assembly to create a constitution that would complete the transition to democracy. At the time we were visiting, Pema told us that Bhutan's constitution was in the final stages of development and would be ratified soon. While we toured Bhutan, we saw voting instructions on telephone poles and in the newspapers, along with orders to participate in the upcoming "practice election" to be held several months after our visit. Pema told us that some older people lacked enthusiasm for the election process because they liked having a benevolent king who made the major decisions for them. However, the younger Bhutanese, especially those who had lived outside the country, supported the changes.

At the time of our visit, data collection on consumer debt, the vigor of the environment, and the health of the people had been completed. The tool to measure and track GNH Index was almost ready. In 2008, the National Assembly passed the final version of the constitution that included the details of the Gross National Happiness Index, which made this new concept measurable and viable for incorporating into the planning process.

The Underbelly of Bhutan's Happiness

Current visitors to Bhutan extol the virtues of GNH without understanding the whole picture. Ten years after my visit in 2007, improvements to Bhutan's quality of life are guided by the king's desire to preserve national identity, traditional values, and the concept of "One Nation, One People," which he decreed in 1989. It sounded good at the time, but in this desire for "one people" lurks the underbelly of Bhutan's lauded GNH.

Surprisingly, I also learned that the Bhutanese government only canvassed full-blooded Drukpas— descendants of the original Tibetan immigrants—to obtain data for the measurement of GNH. At the time we visited, we heard that access to healthcare, higher education, and the better paying jobs were heavily determined by bloodlines and closely linked to citizenship, making it a tough and very unhappy situation for Lhotshampas.

This is the underbelly of Bhutan's quest for GNH among its citizens. Apparently, happiness in Bhutan only applies to *some* people.

Revered Black Neck Cranes from the wall of Punakha Dzong.

CHAPTER 6

Moving Toward Democracy

Bhutan held its first countrywide general election in December 2008, a year after my visit and after the coronation of Fifth King Jigme Khaser Namgyel Wangchuck. I hoped the transition to a democratic constitutional monarchy would help diffuse the internal tensions. The elected members of the new parliament agreed that the conflict between the Drukpas and the Lhotshampas needed to be addressed. The governments of Nepal and Bhutan resolved to negotiate a solution to the refugee situation. Nothing came of it.

In 2013, Bhutan held its second national election and an overwhelming majority voted for Tshering Tobgay to be the new prime minister of Bhutan. He had been the Leader of the Opposition in the National Assembly since the first election in 2008. Based on media interviews and written assessments, Tobgay seemed like a capable leader well grounded in the values expressed in Bhutan's Gross National Happiness Index.

Educated in the United States, Tobgay knows how messy a democracy can be and he has not been shy about admitting the shortcomings of Bhutan's development. As recently as October 2016 at an international meeting, Tobgay told the prime minister of Nepal that Bhutan would take the initiative to resolve the problem of refugees—soon. Much as Tobgay might like to, he cannot act alone as the kings were once able to do. The point has become moot since most of the refugees from the camps in Nepal have been resettled. Some 80,000 refugees settled in major cities in the United States, with the largest populations settling in Texas, North Carolina, Indiana, Georgia, and New York.

By 2016, the World Bank reported good economic progress in Bhutan. The economy relies primarily on tourism, small manufacturing, and the sale of hydroelectricity. Every five-year plan includes an analysis of the problems in the country at the time the government issues a new plan, along with realistic goals for the next five years. In 2013, Bhutan implemented the Eleventh Five-Year Plan, in part addressing labor issues that continue to plague development.

Similarities to Developing African Nations

Bhutan's struggles with its transition to a democracy compare favorably with two African countries where I lived during the late 1960s. In 1964, I attended Malawi's independence ceremony and joined the cries of freedom in a stadium full of new citizens. Kamuzu Hastings Banda became the new president and my Crossroads

Africa team of college students enjoyed dinner with the new cabinet during that momentous summer. The ministers were optimistic about their new nation and seemed capable and confident. By fall, half of the cabinet members were in jail or had left the country in fear for their lives. In 1974, the "savior," Kamuzu Hastings Banda, declared himself "President for Life." The iron-fisted leader who ruled until 1994, crushed the hopes of his people for freedom and prosperity.

The British Protectorate of Tanganyika had acquired its independence from Britain in 1961, and the people had similar high hopes. In 1964, Tanganyika joined with Zanzibar to form the United Republic of Tanzania. As a Peace Corps volunteer in Tanzania, I taught at a girl's secondary school from 1966 through 1967. A leader in the independence movement and the first elected president during that time, Mwalimu Julius Nyerere, tried his best to lead Tanzania forward. I was excited to be a part of this dramatic emergence of a new country, but by my last term of teaching, the government leaders' corruption and greed had begun to undermine the gentle and well-respected Nyerere's efforts. I left Tanzania with a heavy heart.

We in the United States are still uncomfortable with our chaotic democracy after more than 200 years, so it's no surprise that Bhutan struggles to establish a strong democratic foundation. To make profound changes from a monarchy with a benevolent king to the chaos of a democracy in a relatively short time is a delicate and difficult dance.

I am sad that the ethnic clashes have not been resolved in Bhutan, just as I am distraught about my own country's unresolved immigration and racial challenges. What a heavy burden the kings carried for their small country while surrounding nations swirled powerful external forces, precipitating changes and chaos that Bhutan still must deflect. I will be watching Bhutan with the hope that they weather their transition and that all their citizens will be happy. I want this for my own country as well.

A Rare Bird vs. a New Airport

A favorite memory from my tour of Bhutan comes from a clash between progress and birds. We spent a night in the glacial Phobjikha Valley, about 9,800 feet above sea level. This protected area is thirty miles east of Thimphu and separates western and central Bhutan. Government planners saw the need for a second international airport to take the pressure off the one located in Paro. The flat landscape of the Phobjika Valley seemed to be a good option. However, this isolated valley is one of only three places in the world where the sacred and endangered Black-necked Cranes winter.

Bhutanese residents in Phobijkha Valley alerted the airport planners that the long-necked cranes could not avoid the recently installed electrical wires during their take offs and landings and many cranes died. They knew that adding an airport to the valley would devastate the birds. In response to those concerns, the planners eliminated that site from consideration for an airport. The government also buried the electrical wires to protect the birds. As of 2017, Bhutan still only has the one international airport in Paro.

The cranes had left the Phobjikha Valley for the season when we visited, but other birds delighted us. Richard's excellent notes helped me remember that in the Phobjikha area, we saw Lesser Racket-tailed Drongo, Golden-throated Barbet, Striated Bulbul, Black-faced Warbler, White-throated Laughingthrush, Whiskered Yuhinia, and Black-throated Parrotbill, among others. Just reading these unusual bird names, many years after visiting Bhutan, brings back the joy of my trip.

Reflections on Bhutan

When I left Bhutan in a post-trip glow, I wrote in my journal, "I found the country stunningly beautiful and the birds exquisite, measuring up to my highest expectations for a birding trip. As a birder, the care of the environment warms my conservationist's heart. Bhutan is a bright light for me in a world that seems headed in the wrong direction. I was so glad my birding interests led me to an uplifting visit to that wonderful country."

Only later did I discover the complexities that plague the country in spite of the best of intentions. Since then, I have followed Bhutan's progress, especially the efforts to protect this environmental paradise. In his TED talk in 2016, Prime Minister Tobgay stated that 70 percent of the country is still forested, so I am thrilled to know that Bhutan is staying firm on the protection of the environment, regardless of political issues that challenge land use.

The Bhuddism-based culture, the architecture of the *dzongs,* the friendly people in their traditional dress—all of these and more, delighted me every day during my three weeks in Bhutan. More than ten years later, the comments I wrote as I left Bhutan still stand. At the time, I was a novice birder and this birding trip stands out for me as one of the best, even after sixteen international birding trips to twenty different countries. Recollections of encounters with such a range of bird species on high mountain passes, by rushing rivers, in deep valleys, in the tops of trees, and along the steep hillside roads, still bring a smile to my face.

Acknowledgments

More *Than Birding* would not have been possible without the help of many people who paved the way for me. My high school biology teacher, Calvin Foulk, intensified my interest in all living things and helped me organize my thoughts about the natural world. Someone at Pomona College arranged for five students to join Operation Crossroads Africa in 1964, which became a life-changing trip, the first of many international journeys. And I am grateful to President John F. Kennedy who thought the Peace Corps was a worthwhile program. It certainly was for me.

Once I began birding, many people eased my entry into the sport. I am grateful for the guides and staff at Field Guides Birding Tours whose skills and enthusiasm account for my many birding tours with their company. Richard Webster led my Field Guides trips to Bhutan, a country he has returned to often, which was evident in his mastery of the birds and the country. I am grateful to Dave Eschbaugh, past-Executive Director of Portland Audubon Society, whose research assured me that our tour to Antarctica would not harm the environment. Thanks also go to Mark Smith, principle of Mark

Smith Nature Tours, who developed and led my tour to Madagascar.

My fellow travelers have always been generous with their guidance and advice, and I am especially grateful to those who shared their personal photos since capturing good images of birds is a skill I do not possess.

As I roughed out and refined the pieces for this book, my writing group always gave gentle and informed critiques. Thank you all: Barbara Cervantes-Gautsche, Jane Galin, Nancy LaPaglia, Shulamit Lotate, Katy Riker, Ruth Roth, and Nancy Turner.

Throughout the writing, my patient editor, Maureen R. Michelson, made wonderful suggestions for additional inclusions and research, and has coached, cheered and consoled me as needed. Her help has made the book much richer and more informative. The book designer, Sherry Wachter, did an amazing job, especially with the photographs, many of which began as snapshots never intended for a publication.

—HARRIET DENISON
August 2018

www.ingramcontent.com/pod-product-compliance
Lightning Source LLC
Chambersburg PA
CBHW022008100426
42736CB00041B/1011